Modern Critical Interpretations

Willa Cather's
MY ÁNTONIA

Modern Critical Interpretations

These and other titles in preparation

Modern Critical Interpretations

Willa Cather's
MY ÁNTONIA

Edited and with an introduction by
Harold Bloom
Sterling Professor of the Humanities
Yale University

Chelsea House Publishers ◊ *1987*

NEW YORK ◊ NEW HAVEN ◊ PHILADELPHIA

©1987 by Chelsea House Publishers, a division of Chelsea
House Educational Communications, Inc.,
  95 Madison Ave, New York, NY 10016
  345 Whitney Avenue, New Haven, CT 06511
  5014 West Chester Pike, Edgemont, PA 19028

Introduction © 1985 by Harold Bloom

Printed and bound in the United States of America

∞The paper used in this publication meets the minimum
requirements of the American National Standard for
Permanence of Paper for Printed Library Materials, Z39.48–1984.

Library of Congress Cataloging-in-Publication Data

Willa Cather's My Antonia

  (Modern critical interpretations)
  Bibliography: p.
  Includes index.
  1. Cather, Willa, 1873–1947. My Antonia.
I. Bloom, Harold. II. Series.
PS3505.A87M8947   1987   813'.52   86–34325
ISBN 1–55546–035–6 (alk. paper)

Contents

Editor's Note

This book gathers together what I judge to be the best criticism available upon Willa Cather's *My Ántonia*. The critical discussions are reprinted here in the chronological order of their original publication. I am grateful to Daniel Klotz for his aid in researching this volume.

My introduction sets *My Ántonia* and Cather's other masterwork, *A Lost Lady,* in the context of her place in American literary tradition. David Daiches begins the chronological sequence of criticism with a reminder of the technical limitation that Cather accepts by never allowing Ántonia to reveal herself fully or directly to the reader. The dialectic of time and the frontier in the novel is explored by James E. Miller, Jr., while Robert E. Scholes finds in Cather's vision the familiar nineteenth-century American agon between the party of memory and the party of hope.

In Dorothy Van Ghent's reading, *My Ántonia* centers upon the great image of "the plow hieroglyphed on the sun," a metaphor consonant with Wallace Stegner's appreciation of Ántonia herself as an image radiant with nostalgic lyricism. Memory, the novel's obsession and prime resource, is analyzed by Terence Martin as a mode of fulfillment in the book's present time.

Cather's mode of reaching form through perspectivizings of time and space is studied by David Stouck, while Blanche H. Gelfant considers the even subtler perspectivizing of sex in the novel. James E. Miller, Jr., returns with a second essay, this time centering upon *My Ántonia*'s version of the American Dream, of a romance lost in the past.

The fertility rituals of the ancient Greek Eleusinian Mysteries, revived by Cather in the final book of *My Ántonia,* are seen by Evelyn Helmick as giving the novel a mythic reverberation that greatly enhances its power. In this volume's final essay, Deborah G. Lambert analyzes some of *My Ántonia*'s "strange flaws and omissions" as "the consequences of Cather's dilemma as a lesbian writer in a partriarchal society."

Introduction

I

Willa Cather, though now somewhat neglected, has few rivals among the American novelists of this century. Critics and readers frequently regard her as belonging to an earlier time, though she died in 1947. Her best novels were published in the years 1918–31, so that truly she was a novelist of the 1920s, an older contemporary and peer of Hemingway and of Scott Fitzgerald. Unlike them, she did not excel at the short story, though there are some memorable exceptions scattered through her four volumes of tales. Her strength is her novels and particularly, in my judgment, *My Ántonia* (1918), *A Lost Lady* (1923) and *The Professor's House* (1925), fictions worthy of a disciple of Flaubert and Henry James. Equally beautiful and achieved, but rather less central, are the subsequent historical novels, the very popular *Death Comes for the Archbishop* (1927) and *Shadows on the Rock* (1931). Her second novel, *O Pioneers!* (1913), is only just short of the eminence of this grand sequence. Six permanent novels is a remarkable number for a modern American writer; I can think only of Faulkner as Cather's match in this respect, since he wrote six truly enduring novels, all published during his great decade, 1929–39.

Cather's remoteness from the fictive universe of Fitzgerald, Hemingway and Faulkner is palpable, though all of them shared her nostalgia for an older America. She appears, at first, to have no aesthetic affinities with her younger contemporaries. We associate her instead with Sarah Orne Jewett, about whom she wrote a loving essay, or even with Edith Wharton, whom she scarcely resembles. Cather's mode of engaging with the psychic realities of post-World War I America is more oblique than Fitzgerald's or Hemingway's, but it is just as apposite a representation of the era's malaise. The short novel, *A Lost Lady* (1923), is not out of its aesthetic context when we read it in the company of *The Waste Land, The*

1

Comedian as the Letter C, The Sun Also Rises, The Great Gatsby, and *An American Tragedy.* Subtler and gentler than any of these, *A Lost Lady* elegizes just as profoundly a lost radiance or harmony, a defeat of a peculiarly American dream of innocence, grace, hope.

II

Henry James, Cather's guide both as critic and novelist, died in England early in 1916. The year before, replying to H. G. Wells, after being satirized by him, James wrote a famous credo: "Art *makes* life, makes interest, makes importance." This is Cather's faith also. One hears the voice of James when, in her essay "On the Art of Fiction," she writes: "Any first-rate novel or story must have in it the strength of a dozen fairly good stories that have been sacrificed to it." Those sacrifices of possibility upon the altar of form were the ritual acts of Cather's quite Paterian religion of art, too easily misread as a growing religiosity by many critics commenting upon *Death Comes for the Archbishop.* Herself a belated Aesthete, Cather emulated a familiar pattern of being attracted by the aura and not the substance of Roman Catholicism. New Mexico, and not Rome, is her place of the spirit, a spirit of the archaic and not of the supernatural.

Cather's social attitudes were altogether archaic. She shared a kind of Populist anti-Semitism with many American writers of her own generation and the next: Sherwood Anderson, Theodore Dreiser, Ezra Pound, Thomas Wolfe, even Hemingway and Fitzgerald. Her own version of anti-Semitism is curiously marked by her related aversion to heterosexuality. She had lost her first companion, Isabelle McClung, to a Jewish violinist, Jan Hambourg, and the Jewish figures in her fiction clearly represent the aggressivity of male sexuality. *The Professor's House* is marred by the gratuitous identification of the commercial exploitation of Cather's beloved West with Marcellus, the Professor's Jewish son-in-law. Doubtless, Cather's most unfortunate piece of writing was her notorious essay in 1914, "Potash and Perlmutter," in which she lamented, mock-heroically, that New York City was becoming too Jewish. Perhaps she was learning the lesson of the master again, since she is repeating, in a lighter tone, the complaint of Henry James in *The American Scene* (1907). She repeated her own distaste for "Jewish critics," tainted as they were by Freud, in the essay on Sarah Orne Jewett written quite late in her career, provoking Lionel Trilling to the just accusation that she had become a mere defender of gentility, mystically concerned with pots and pans.

This dark side of Cather, though hardly a value in itself, would not much matter except that it seeped into her fiction as a systemic resentment of her own era. Nietzsche, analyzing resentment, might be writing of Cather. Freud, analyzing the relation between paranoia and homosexuality, might be writing of her also. I am wary of being reductive in such observations, and someone perpetually mugged by feminist critics as "the Patriarchal critic" is too battered to desire any further polemic. Cather, in my judgment, is aesthetically strongest and most persuasive in her loving depiction of her heroines and of Ántonia and the lost lady, Mrs. Forrester, in particular. She resembles Thomas Hardy in absolutely nothing, except in the remarkable ability to seduce the reader into joining the novelist at falling in love with the heroine. I am haunted by memories of having fallen in love with Marty South in *The Woodlanders,* and with Ántonia and Mrs. Forrester, when I was a boy of fifteen. Rereading *My Ántonia* and *A Lost Lady,* now at fifty-four, I find that the love renews itself. I doubt that I am falling again into what my late and honored teacher, William K. Wimsatt, named as the Affective Fallacy, since love for a woman made up out of words is necessarily a cognitive affair.

Cather's strength at representation gives us Jim Burden and Niel Herbert as her clear surrogates, unrealized perhaps as figures of sexual life, but forcefully conveyed as figures of capable imagination, capable above all of apprehending and transmitting the extraordinary actuality and visionary intensity of Ántonia and Mrs. Forrester. Like her masters, James and Pater, Cather had made her supposed deficiency into her strength, fulfilling the overt program of Emersonian self-reliance. But nothing is got for nothing, Emerson also indicated, and Cather, again like James and Pater, suffered the reverse side of the law of Compensation. The flaws, aesthetic and human, are there, even in *My Ántonia, A Lost Lady* and *The Professor's House,* but they scarcely diminish the beauty and dignity of three profound studies of American nostalgias.

III

Cather is hardly the only vital American novelist to have misread creatively the spirit of his or her own work. Her essential imaginative knowledge was of loss, which she interpreted temporally, though her loss was aboriginal, in the Romantic mode of Wordsworth, Emerson and all their varied descendants. The glory that had passed away belonged not to the pioneers but to her own transparent eyeball, her own original relation to the universe. Rhetorically, she manifests this knowledge, which frequently is at odds with her overt thematicism. Here is Jim Burden's first shared moment with Ántonia, when they both were little children:

> We sat down and made a nest in the long red grass. Yulka curled up like a baby rabbit and played with a grasshopper. Ántonia pointed up to the sky and questioned me with her glance. I gave her the word, but she was not satisfied and pointed to my eyes. I told her, and she repeated the word, making it sound like "ice." She pointed up to the sky, then to my eyes, then back to the sky, with movements so quick and impulsive that she distracted me, and I had no idea what she wanted. She got up on her knees and wrung her hands. She pointed to her own eyes and shook her head, then to mine and to the sky, nodding violently.
>
> "Oh," I exclaimed, "blue; blue sky."
>
> She clapped her hands and murmured, "Blue sky, blue eyes," as if it amused her. While we snuggled down there out of the wind, she learned a score of words. She was quick, and very eager. We were so deep in the grass that we could see nothing but the blue sky over us and the gold tree in front of us. It was wonderfully pleasant. After Ántonia had said the new words over and over, she wanted to give me a little chased silver ring she wore on her middle finger. When she coaxed and insisted, I repulsed her quite sternly. I didn't want her ring, and I felt there was something reckless and extravagant about her wishing to give it away to a boy she had never seen before. No wonder Krajiek got the better of these people, if this was how they behaved.

One imagines that Turgenev would have admired this, and it would not be out of place inserted in his *A Sportman's Sketchbook*. Its naturalistic simplicity is deceptive. Wallace Stevens, in a letter of 1940, observed of Cather: "you may think she is more or less formless. Nevertheless, we have nothing better than she is. She takes so much pains to conceal her sophistication that it is easy to miss her quality." The quality here is partly manifested by an exuberance of trope and a precision of diction, both in the service of a fresh American myth of origin. Nesting and curling up in an embowered world of baby rabbits and grasshoppers, the children are at home in a universe of "blue sky, blue eyes." Heaven and earth come together, where vision confronts only the gold of trees. Ántonia, offering the fullness of a symbolic union to him, is rebuffed partly by the boy's shyness, and partly by Cather's own proleptic fear that the reckless gener-osity of the pioneer is doomed to exploitation. Yet the passage's deepest intimation is that Jim, though falling in love with Ántonia, is constrained by an inner recalcitrance, which the reader is free to interpret in several ways, none of which need exclude the others.

This is Cather in the spring tide of her imagination. In her vision's early fall, we find ourselves regarding her lost lady, Mrs. Forrester, and we are comforted, as the boy Niel Herbert is, "in the quick recognition of her eyes, in the living quality of her voice itself." The book's splendor is that, like Mrs. Forrester's laughter, "it often told you a great deal that was both too direct and too elusive for words." As John Hollander shrewdly notes, Mrs. Forrester does not become a lost lady in any social or moral sense, but imaginatively she is transformed into Niel's "long-lost lady." Lost or refound, she is "his" always, even as Ántonia always remains Jim Burden's "my Ántonia." In her ability to suggest a love that is permanent, life-enhancing, and in no way possessive, Cather touches the farthest limit of her own strength as a novelist. If one could choose a single passage from all her work, it would be the Paterian epiphany or privileged mo-ment in which Mrs. Forrester's image returned to Niel as "a bright, imper-sonal memory." Pater ought to have lived to have read this marvelous in-stance of the art he had celebrated and helped to stimulate in Cather:

> Her eyes, when they laughed for a moment into one's own, seemed to provide a wild delight that he had not found in life. "I know where it is," they seemed to say, "I could show you!" He would like to call up the shade of the young Mrs. Forrester, as the witch of Endor called up Samuel's, and challenge it, de-mand the secret of that ardour; ask her whether she had really found some ever-blooming, ever-burning, ever-piercing joy, or whether it was all fine play-acting. Probably she had found no more than another; but she had always the power of sug-gesting things much lovelier than herself, as the perfume of a single flower may call up the whole sweetness of spring.

It is the perfection of Cather's difficult art, when that art was most balanced and paced, and Mrs. Forrester here is the emblem of that perfec-tion. Cather's fiction, at its frequent best, also suggests things much love-lier than itself. The reader, demanding the secret of Cather's ardour, learns not to challenge what may be remarkably fine play-acting, since Cather's feigning sometimes does persuade him that really she had found some per-petual joy.

Decline of the West

David Daiches

My Ántonia, which appeared in 1918, is another story of pioneering life in Nebraska. Like *O Pioneers!* it contains autobiographical elements—the heroine was suggested by "a Bohemian girl who was good to me when I was a child"—and is concerned with the conflict between memory and desire, nostalgia and ambition, in the immigrant. The European background, which lies behind the book like a fascinating mystery, is both attractive and disturbing: the picturesque and feudal Bohemia for which Mr. Shimerda languishes is but one aspect of a background which includes the horror of the Russian scene where famished wolves pursue a bridal party returning home during the night. Yet, for all the tensions between the Old World and the New to be found in this novel as in so many of the others, the central theme is neither the struggle of the pioneer nor the conflict between generations, but the development and self-discovery of the heroine. This suggests a structure like that of *The Song of the Lark;* but in fact the book is organized much more like *O Pioneers!* We do not follow the heroine's career in the anxious detail we find in the preceding novel. Although Willa Cather did not at the time agree with Mr. Heinemann's criticism of *The Song of the Lark* and its "full-blooded method," she tells us that "when the next book, *My Ántonia,* came along, quite of itself and with no direction from me, it took the road of *O Pioneers!*—not the road of *The Song of the Lark.*"

The story is told in the first person by Jim Burden, childhood friend

From *Willa Cather: A Critical Introduction.* © 1951 by Cornell University. Cornell University Press, 1951.

of the heroine and now "legal counsel for one of the great Western railways." This device gives proper voice to the autobiographical impulse which lies behind much of the book; but it has its dangers. No observer, however knowing and sympathetic, can tell the full story of the development of a character like Ántonia. A character who is constantly talked about, described, and discussed but who never reveals herself fully and directly to the reader tends to become the kind of symbol the observer wants to make of her, an objectification of the observer's emotions, and this in large measure does happen to Ántonia. Her growth, development, and final adjustment is a vast symbolic progress, interesting less for what it is than for what it can be made to mean.

This is in some degree true also of Alexandra Bergson in *O Pioneers!*, who emerges at the end of the book as a kind of Earth Goddess symbolic of what the pioneers had achieved on the Nebraska plains. There is an epic quality in *O Pioneers!* which makes one resent the intrusion of incidents drawn to a smaller scale. That epic quality is lacking in *My Ántonia:* the cultivation of the land is not something *achieved* by Ántonia, but something in which she submerges herself in order to attain salvation. She ends as the ideal wife and mother, bound to the farming life, more devoted than ever to the open spaces: but it is not she who has made that life possible or tamed those open spaces so much as it is that life and those spaces which have saved her.

Throughout the book the narrator's sensibility takes control; and this raises problems which Willa Cather is never quite able to solve. The narrator's development goes on side by side with Ántonia's: indeed, we sometimes lose sight of Ántonia for long stretches at a time, while we can never lose sight of the narrator. Miss Cather tries to solve this problem by emphasizing that the book's title is *My Ántonia:* this is not just the story of Ántonia, but of Ántonia as she impinged on a number of other significant characters. She goes out of the way to use the adjective "my" in talking of Ántonia with reference not only to the narrator but also to other characters—to her father, who first uses the phrase, and to Mrs. Steavens, for example. And yet we cannot say that this is a story of what Ántonia meant to a selected number of other characters of the book: though there are elements in the story which suggest this, the organization as a whole tends to present Ántonia as a symbolic figure in her own right rather than as a character with special meaning for particular individuals.

Some of these points may be made clearer by a more detailed discussion of the story. It opens with the arrival of Jim Burden, the narrator, at his grandparents' farm in Nebraska: he has been sent there from Virginia at the age of ten on the death of his parents (Willa Cather, too, had come from Virginia to Nebraska as a child). The Shimerdas arrive from Bohemia at the same time to settle in a raw neighboring farm whose ill-kept sod house provides a sad contrast to the fine wooden house of Jim's grandparents. The Shimerdas were the first Bohemian family to come to that part of the country. "They could not speak enough English to ask for advice, or even to make their most pressing wants known." Mr. Shimerda, cultured, melancholy, completely lost in this rough new country, lives in the past, having lost the will to adjust, and ends by committing suicide. His wife, an altogether less refined and coarser person, complains and bullies her way along until, with the assistance of neighbors, her situation improves. His nineteen-year-old son Ambrosch, to advance whose fortunes Mrs. Shimerda had insisted on emigrating to America, is sullen, insensitive, hard-working, and cunning. There is another son, who is mentally deficient and plays but a small part in the story. Then there is Ántonia, four years older than Jim, with brown hair, brown skin, golden-brown eyes, and a personality rich enough to make up for all deficiencies in other members of her family. Ántonia has a younger sister, Yulka, whose role is quite minor.

The relation between the Burdens and the Shimerdas is at the beginning that of relatively prosperous neighbors to a distressed immigrant family. The Shimerdas had not been fairly dealt with by the Bohemian homesteader from whom they had bought their land and sod house, and they found conditions appalling on arrival. Had it not been for the assistance of the Burdens they would not have survived their first winter in Nebraska. Jim and Ántonia are thrown together from the beginning, and from the beginning Ántonia, in spite of her fragmentary English and humbler circumstances, is the dominating character. Together they explore the countryside and learn to know and love the Nebraska plains. Incidents are contrived by the author to bring out different aspects of the Nebraska scene and atmosphere, and there is some impressive descriptive writing.

There are episodes in this first part of the book that have little if any relation to the story of Ántonia's development—the story of the two Russians, Peter and Pavel, for example. Mr. Shimerda, who could understand their language, made friends with them, but soon afterward Pavel died, and on his deathbed he told the terrible story of how as a young man in Russia he had thrown a bride and groom off a sledge to the pursuing wolves in order to save himself from certain death. This is a remarkable little inset story, but its relation to the novel as a whole is somewhat uncertain. It was soon after the death of Pavel and the subsequent departure of

Peter that Mr. Shimerda committed suicide. By this time it was midwinter, and the atmosphere of the frozen landscape is effectively employed to emphasize the pity and horror of this death from homesickness.

Mr. Shimerda had hoped to see Ántonia get a good American education, but after his death she took her place as one of the workers on the farm, to which she devoted all her time.

> When the sun was dropping low, Ántonia came up the big south draw with her team. How much older she had grown in eight months! She had come to us a child, and now she was a tall, strong young girl, although her fifteenth birthday had just slipped by. I ran out and met her as she brought her horses up to the windmill to water them. She wore the boots her father had so thoughtfully taken off before he shot himself, and his old fur cap. Her outgrown cotton dress switched about her calves, over the boot-tops. She kept her sleeves rolled up all day, and her arms and throat were burned as brown as a sailor's. Her neck came up strongly out of her shoulders, like the bole of a tree out of the turf. One sees that draught-horse neck among the peasant women in all old countries.

For all her devotion to her father's memory, Mr. Shimerda's mantle does not fall on Ántonia, but rather on Jim, who responds to the suggestion of a rich European culture lying behind his melancholy. This is the first of a series of influences that lead him eventually to the university and a professional career in the East, yet in a profound if indirect way it draws him closer to Ántonia.

Jim goes to school while Ántonia works on the farm:

> "I came to ask you something, Tony. Grandmother wants to know if you can't go to the term of school that begins next week over at the sod school-house. She says there's a good teacher, and you'd learn a lot."
>
> Ántonia stood up, lifting and dropping her shoulders as if they were stiff. "I ain't got time to learn. I can work like mans now. My mother can't say no more how Ambrosch do all and nobody to help him. I can work as much as him. School is all right for little boys. I help make this land one good farm."
>
> She clucked to her team and started for the barn. I walked beside her, feeling vexed. Was she going to grow up boastful like her mother, I wondered? Before we reached the stable, I

felt something tense in her silence, and glancing up I saw that she was crying. She turned her face from me and looked off at the red streak of dying light, over the dark prairie.

I climbed up into the loft and threw down the hay for her, while she unharnessed her team. We walked slowly back toward the house. Ambrosch had come in from the north quarter, and was watering his oxen at the tank.

Ántonia took my hand. "Sometime you will tell me all those nice things you learn at the school, won't you, Jimmy?" she asked with a sudden rush of feeling in her voice. "My father, he went much to school. He know a great deal; how to make the fine cloth like what you not got here. He play horn and violin, and he read so many books that the priests in Bohemie come to talk to him. You won't forget my father, Jim?"

"No," I said, "I will never forget him."

The first section of *My Ántonia* ends with a brilliant summer scene. Ántonia and Jim watch an electric storm from the slanting roof of the Burdens' chicken house:

The thunder was loud and metallic, like the rattle of sheet iron, and the lightning broke in great zigzags across the heavens, making everything stand out and come close to us for a moment. Half the sky was chequered with black thunderheads, but all the west was luminous and clear: in the lightning flashes it looked like deep blue water, with the sheen of moonlight on it; and the mottled part of the sky was like marble pavement, like the quay of some splendid seacoast city, doomed to destruction. Great warm splashes of rain fell on our upturned faces. One black cloud, no bigger than a little boat, drifted out into the clear space unattended, and kept moving westward. All about us we could hear the felty beat of the raindrops on the soft dust of the farmyard. Grandmother came to the door and said it was late, and we would get wet out there.

"In a minute we come," Ántonia called back to her. "I like your grandmother, and all things here," she sighed. "I wish my papa live to see this summer. I wish no winter ever come again."

"It will be summer a long while yet," I reassured her. "Why aren't you always nice like this, Tony?"

"How nice?"

"Why, just like this; like yourself. Why do you all the time try to be like Ambrosch?"

She put her arms under her head and lay back, looking up at the sky. "If I live here, like you, that is different. Things will be easy for you. But they will be hard for us."

After three years on the farm Jim and his grandparents move to the "clean, well-planted little prairie town" of Black Hawk. The second section of the book concerns life in Black Hawk. Ántonia has to be brought in, so Miss Cather contrives to have her engaged as a cook by the Harlings, the family who live next door to the Burdens in their new home. It is, perhaps, a rather artificial device to move the heroine temporarily into the narrator's town in order to keep her under his eye, but the sequence of events which brings this about is not improbable in terms of the story as told. What is more dubious is the relation of this whole section of the novel to the main theme of the story. It is in itself a brilliantly written section. Life in the small prairie town is described with a cunning eye for the significant detail, and a fine emotional rhythm runs through the whole. The daughters of the immigrant (mostly Swedish) farmers in the country round about have come into town to get positions as maids and thereby help their families to improve their economic position: Jim and Tony move happily in these humble circles, whose healthy gaiety is sharply contrasted with the narrow stuffiness of the tradespeople and their families.

> Those girls had grown up in the first bitter-hard times, and had got little schooling themselves. But the younger brothers and sisters, for whom they made such sacrifices and who have had "advantages," never seem to me, when I meet them now, half as interesting or as well educated. The older girls, who helped to break up the wild sod, learned so much from life, from poverty, from their mothers and grandmothers; they had all, like Ántonia, been early awakened and made observant by coming at a tender age from an old country to a new.
>
> I can remember a score of these country girls who were in service in Black Hawk during the few years I lived there, and I can remember something unusual and engaging about each of them. Physically they were almost a race apart, and out-of-door work had given them a vigour which, when they got over their first shyness on coming to town, developed into a positive carriage and freedom of movement, and made them conspicuous among Black Hawk women.

The feeling that it is the imaginative immigrant and not the stuffy conventional American who is responsible for the country's greatness recurs again and again in Miss Cather's novels:

> The daughters of Black Hawk merchants had a confident, unenquiring belief that they were "refined," and that the country girls, who "worked out," were not. The American farmers in our country were quite as hard-pressed as their neighbours from other countries. All alike had come to Nebraska with little capital and no knowledge of the soil they must subdue. All had borrowed money on their land. But no matter in what straits the Pennsylvanian or Virginian found himself, he would not let his daughters go out into service. Unless his girls could teach a country school, they sat at home in poverty.
>
> The Bohemian and Scandinavian girls could not get positions as teachers, because they had no opportunity to learn the language. Determined to help in the struggle to clear the homestead from debt, they had no alternative but to go into service. . . . But every one of them did what she had set out to do, and sent home those hard-earned dollars. The girls I knew were always helping to pay for ploughs and reapers, broodsows, or steers to fatten.
>
> One result of this family solidarity was that the foreign farmers in our country were the first to become prosperous. After the fathers were out of debt, the daughters married the sons of neighbours—usually of like nationality—and the girls who once worked in Black Hawk kitchens are to-day managing big farms and fine families of their own; their children are better off than the children of the town women they used to serve.
>
> I thought the attitude of the town people toward these girls very stupid. If I told my schoolmates that Lena Lingard's grandfather was a clergyman, and much respected in Norway, they looked at me blankly. What did it matter? All foreigners were ignorant people who couldn't speak English. There was not a man in Black Hawk who had the intelligence or cultivation, much less the personal distinction, of Ántonia's father. Yet people saw no difference between her and the three Marys; they were all Bohemians, all "hired girls."
>
> I always knew I should live long enough to see my country girls come into their own, and I have.

A passage such as this is not the sociological digression it might at first sight seem: it helps to set the emotional tone of this section of the novel and is not unrelated to the main theme of Ántonia's development. Yet there is much in the description of life in Black Hawk which is not part of this pattern, but of the quite different pattern of the development and career of Jim Burden. These final years at high school before moving on to the University of Nebraska were of course very significant in Jim's career, as they were in that of Miss Cather, who followed a similar progress. Ántonia plays a very minor part in this section, while the gradually maturing Jim looks out in excitement and growing understanding on the social scene in Black Hawk. Is it that Jim is fitting himself to be the ideal observer of Ántonia? That seems to be the only way in which this part of the novel can be structurally justified.

But, as we have noted, the section considered by itself is a remarkable piece of writing. The account of the Harling family, the extraordinary story of Mr. and Mrs. Cutter, scenes at the Boys' Home ("the best hotel on our branch of the Burlington"), the Saturday night dances in the tent set up on the vacant lot, the blind Negro pianist playing at the hotel, and through it all the good-humored and purposeful "hired girls" moving with a freedom and vitality that put the middle-class females of Black Hawk to shame—in this kind of descriptive writing Miss Cather was doing for her part of the country something of what Sarah Orne Jewett had done for New England. There is the flavor of a region and of a community here, and we can see why, in turning to this phase of her story, Willa Cather occasionally lost sight of her main theme.

A scene such as this, in the hotel, has real flavor to it:

> When I stole into the parlour, Anson Kirkpatrick, Marshall Field's man, was at the piano, playing airs from a musical comedy then running in Chicago. He was a dapper little Irishman, very vain, homely as a monkey, with friends everywhere, and a sweetheart in every port, like a sailor. I did not know all the men who were sitting about, but I recognized a furniture salesman from Kansas City, a drug man, and Willy O'Reilly, who travelled for a jewellery house and sold musical instruments. The talk was all about good and bad hotels, actors and actresses and musical prodigies. I learned that Mrs. Gardener had gone to Omaha to hear Booth and Barrett, who were to play there next week, and that Mary Anderson was having a great success in "A Winter's Tale," in London.

Or consider this winter scene, which can be set beside the opening scene in *O Pioneers!*:

> If I loitered on the playground after school, or went to the post-office for the mail and lingered to hear the gossip about the cigar-stand, it would be growing dark by the time I came home. The sun was gone; the frozen streets stretched long and blue before me; the lights were shining pale in kitchen windows, and I could smell the suppers cooking as I passed. Few people were abroad, and each one of them was hurrying toward a fire. The glowing stoves in the houses were like magnets. When one passed an old man, one could see nothing of his face but a red nose sticking out between a frosted beard and a long plush cap. The young men capered along with their hands in their pockets, and sometimes tried a slide on the icy sidewalk. The children, in their bright hoods and comforters, never walked, but always ran from the moment they left their door, beating their mittens against their sides. When I got as far as the Methodist Church, I was about halfway home. I can remember how glad I was when there happened to be a light in the church, and the painted glass window shone out at us as we came along the frozen street. In the winter bleakness a hunger for colour came over people, like the Laplander's craving for fats and sugar. Without knowing why, we used to linger on the sidewalk outside the church when the lamps were lighted early for choir practice or prayer-meeting, shivering and talking until our feet were like lumps of ice. The crude reds and greens and blues of that coloured glass held us there.

In the third section of the novel we lose sight of Ántonia almost completely. This section deals with Jim Burden at the University of Nebraska, his mild affair with Lena Lingard, one of the Swedish farm girls who has come to the city and set up as a dressmaker, and his decision to continue his studies at Harvard. Jim and his development provide the chief center of interest here, and one suspects that Miss Cather is drawing on her own experiences at the University of Nebraska. The high point of this section is an account of a performance of *Camille*, to which Jim takes Lena. The part of Marguerite was taken by a battered old actress, and in many other respects the performance lacked distinction, but for both Jim and Lena this performance of *Camille* by a rather run-down touring company in Lincoln, Nebraska, was one of the great and critical experiences of their lives.

In the fourth section Jim, going home from Harvard in the summer vacation, learns of Ántonia's fate. She had fallen in love with a railroad conductor and gone off to Denver to marry him: but he had not married her, for, unknown to her, he had already lost his job, and he ran off to Mexico leaving her pregnant. Ántonia goes back to her brother's farm subdued but determined to work once again on the land. Jim learns all the details, including the birth of Ántonia's baby, from Mrs. Steavens, who rents the Burdens' old farm. He goes out to see Ántonia and finds her in the fields, shocking wheat: "She was thinner than I had ever seen her, and looked as Mrs. Steavens said, 'worked down,' but there was a new kind of strength in the gravity of her face, and her colour still gave her that look of deep-seated health and ardour. Still? Why, it flashed across me that though so much had happened in her life and in mine, she was barely twenty-four years old."

She tells him that she would always be miserable in a city. "I'd die of lonesomeness. I like to be where I know every stack and tree, and where all the ground is friendly." The Nebraska fields where she and Jim ran about as children now present themselves as the means of her salvation. And yet this rooting of herself in the American soil—a process hastened by her misfortune—is not achieved at the expense of repudiating her European past. They talk of her father. "He's been dead all these years," Ántonia tells Jim, "and yet he is more real to me than almost anybody else. He never goes out of my life. I talk to him and consult him all the time. The older I grow, the better I know him and the more I understand him." This section ends on a note of hope:

> As we walked homeward across the fields, the sun dropped and lay like a great golden globe in the low west. While it hung there, the moon rose in the east, as big as a cart-wheel, pale silver and streaked with rose colour, thin as a bubble or a ghost-moon. For five, perhaps ten minutes, the two luminaries confronted each other across the level land, resting on opposite edges of the world.
>
> In that singular light every little tree and shock of wheat, every sunflower stalk and clump of snow-on-the-mountain, drew itself up high and pointed; the very clods and furrows in the fields seemed to stand up sharply. I felt the old pull of the earth, the solemn magic that comes out of those fields at nightfall. I wished I could be a little boy again, and that my way could end there.

Finally, Jim joins the company of Ántonia's friendly ghosts:

> "I'll come back," I said earnestly, through the soft, intrusive darkness.
>
> "Perhaps you will"—I felt rather than saw her smile. "But even if you don't, you're here, like my father. So I won't be lonesome."
>
> As I went back alone over that familiar road, I could almost believe that a boy and girl ran along beside me, as our shadows used to do, laughing and whispering to each other in the grass.

Perhaps the book ought to have ended here, with Ántonia left alone in the field in the gathering darkness. The concluding section, which redeems Ántonia to a conventional happy ending, kills altogether that note of implicit tragedy that had been sounded in the earlier part of the novel. Yet the conclusion can be justified: it has an appropriate symbolic quality, and the return to Bohemia implied in Ántonia's marriage to a Bohemian immigrant and raising a family who speak only Czech at home resolves an important aspect of the novel's theme.

The final section takes place twenty years later, when Jim returns to the scenes of his childhood and visits Ántonia. "I heard of her from time to time; that she married, very soon after I last saw her, a young Bohemian, a cousin of Anton Jellinek; that they were poor, and had a large family." When he visits her, surrounded by a large family, he can see at once that she has found her proper function as housewife and mother on a Nebraska farm:

> I lay awake for a long while, until the slow-moving moon passed my window on its way up the heavens. I was thinking about Ántonia and her children; about Anna's solicitude for her, Ambrosch's grave affection, Leo's jealous, animal little love. That moment, when they all came tumbling out of the cave into the light, was a sight any man might have come far to see. Ántonia had always been one to leave images in the mind that did not fade—that grew stronger with time. In my memory there was a succession of such pictures fixed there like the old woodcuts of one's first primer: Ántonia kicking her bare legs against the sides of my pony when we came home in triumph with our snake; Ántonia in her black shawl and fur cap, as she stood by her father's grave in the snowstorm; Ántonia coming in with her work-team along the evening skyline.

She lent herself to immemorial human attitudes which we recognize by instinct as universal and true. I had not been mistaken. She was a battered woman now, not a lovely girl; but she still had that something which fires the imagination, could still stop one's breath for a moment by a look or gesture that somehow revealed the meaning in common things. She had only to stand in the orchard, to put her hand on a little crab tree and look up at the apples, to make you feel the goodness of planting and tending and harvesting at last. All the strong things of her heart came out in her body, that had been so tireless in serving generous emotions.

It was no wonder that her sons stood tall and straight. She was a rich mine of life, like the founders of early races.

Jim meets Ántonia's husband, a lively, humorous, dependable Czech, a man more fitted by temperament for the gay life of cities than life on a lonely farm.

I could see the little chap, sitting here every evening by the windmill, nursing his pipe and listening to the silence; the wheeze of the pump, the grunting of the pigs, an occasional squawking when the hens were disturbed by a rat. It did rather seem to me that Cuzak had been made the instrument of Ántonia's special mission. This was a fine life, certainly, but it wasn't the kind of life he had wanted to live. I wondered whether the life that was right for one was ever right for two!

Before he leaves, Jim walks out over the familiar countryside:

This was the road over which Ántonia and I came on that night when we got off the train at Black Hawk and were bedded down in the straw, wondering children, being taken we knew not whither. I had only to close my eyes to hear the rumbling of the wagons in the dark, and to be again overcome by that obliterating strangeness. The feelings of that night were so near that I could reach out and touch them with my hand. I had the sense of coming home to myself, and of having found out what a little circle man's experience is. For Ántonia and for me, this had been the road of Destiny; had taken us to those early accidents of fortune which predetermined for us all that we can ever be. Now I understood that the same road was to bring us together again. Whatever we had missed, we possessed together the precious, the incommunicable past.

The symbolism seems a little uncertain at the conclusion. The final suggestion that this is the story of Jim and Ántonia and their relations is not really borne out by the story as it has developed. It begins as that, but later the strands separate until we have three main themes all going—the history of Ántonia, the history of Jim, and scenes of Nebraska life. It seems that the autobiographical impulse that redeemed Willa Cather from what she later considered the barren artfulness of *Alexander's Bridge* had its own dangers and was responsible for the abundance of interesting but not wholly dominated material which is to be found in *My Ántonia* as in *O Pioneers!*. These two novels are in many respects more alike than any other two of her books: both show vitality, liveliness, and a fine descriptive gift; both show a remarkable ability to project characters and incidents as symbols; but in both the variety of material is not fully integrated with the main theme, and autobiography or regional curiosity sometimes leads the story astray. A flawed novel full of life and interest and possessing a powerful emotional rhythm in spite of its imperfect structural pattern is not, however, a mean achievement, and *My Ántonia* will long be read with pleasure and excitement.

My Ántonia: A Frontier Drama of Time

James E. Miller, Jr.

Critics of Willa Cather have long been confronted with the baffling persistence in popularity of a novel apparently defective in structure. *My Ántonia* may well turn out to be Willa Cather's most fondly remembered and best loved novel, while the perfectly shaped, brilliantly executed *A Lost Lady* continues unread. It does seem strange that one who wanted to unclutter the novel by throwing the furniture out the window should have bungled so badly the structure of one of her most important works.

René Rapin blames Cather for transplanting Ántonia from the country to Black Hawk: "only in her own natural habitat can she hold our attention and capture our emotion." And Rapin censures Cather severely for losing sight of Ántonia completely in the closing books of the novel. David Daiches discovers the source of the defect in Cather's point of view. The "narrator's sensibility," he says, "takes control; and this raises problems which Willa Cather is never quite able to solve." Like Daiches, E. K. Brown is disturbed by the disappearance of Ántonia for pages at a time, and says in the novel's defense: "Everything in the book is there to convey a feeling, not to tell a story, not to establish a social philosophy, not even to animate a group of characters."

Most critics, like Brown, have felt the unified emotional impact of *My Ántonia* and have grappled with the puzzling problem of the book's actual lack of consistent central action or unbroken character portrayal. It is indeed a fine creative achievement to give the effect of unity when there

From *American Quarterly* 10, no. 4 (Winter 1958). © 1958 by the American Studies Association.

apparently is none, and there are those who would claim that the nature of Cather's accomplishment is beyond the critic's understanding, an inscrutable mystery of the artist's miraculous creative process.

The action in *My Ántonia* is episodic, lacks focus and abounds in irrelevancies (consider the inserted wolf-story of Pavel and Peter, for example). Indeed, there is in the novel no plot in the accepted sense of the word. And further, there is not, as there usually is in the plotless story, a character who remains consistently on stage to dominate the obscurely related events. In the second and third books, entitled respectively "The Hired Girls" and "Lena Lingard," Ántonia fades gradually but completely from view, and the reader becomes engrossed, finally, in the excitingly sensual but abortive relationship of the narrator, Jim Burden, and the voluptuous hired girl turned seamstress, Lena Lingard.

But there is that quality of evoked feeling which penetrates the pages of the book, inhering even in the scenes omitting Ántonia, and which gathers finally to a profound and singular focus which constitutes the emotional unity of the book. We sense what we cannot detect—structural elements subtly at work reinforcing and sharpening the aroused feeling.

Jim Burden's assertion in the "Introduction" that he supposes the manuscript he has written "hasn't any form" should not deceive the reader too readily. He also states of Ántonia, "I simply wrote down pretty much all that her name recalls to me." If these confessions reveal that neither action nor character gives unity to the novel, they also suggest, indirectly, that a feeling—the emotion attached to Ántonia's name—informs the novel structurally. When Jim Burden, dissatisfied with "Ántonia" as his title, prefixes the "My," he is informing the reader in advance that the book is *not* about the real Ántonia, but rather about Ántonia as personal and poignant symbol. For Jim, Ántonia becomes symbolic of the undeviating cyclic nature of all life: Ántonia is the insistent reminder that it is the tragic nature of time to bring life to fruition through hardship and struggle only to precipitate the decline and, ultimately, death, but not without first making significant provision for new life to follow, flower and fall. The poignancy lies in the inability of the frail human being to rescue and retain any stage, no matter how beautiful or blissful, of his precious cycle. When Jim Burden asserts at the close of *My Ántonia* that he and Ántonia "possess" the "incommunicable past," he does not convince even himself. It is precisely this emotional conviction that neither they nor anyone else can possess the past, that the past is absolutely and irrevocably "incommunicable" even to those who lived it—which constitutes the novel's unity.

The "feeling" of *My Ántonia* is not the divorced and remote and discomforting "feeling" of the author, nor the displayed or dramatized "feel-ing" of a character, but the evoked feeling of the reader. And the element in the novel which produces and controls this feeling exists in the sensibil-ity of the narrator, Jim Burden. It is in the drama of his awakening con-sciousness, of his growing awareness, that the emotional structure of the novel may be discovered.

It is Jim Burden's sensibility which imposes form on *My Ántonia* and, by that form, shapes in the reader a sharpened awareness of cyclic fate that is the human destiny. The sense of cyclic fate finds expression first in an obsessive engagement with the colorful, somber, and varied seasons of the year, next in an unfolding realization of the immutable and successive phases of human life, and, finally, in an engrossing but bewildering en-counter with the hierarchic stages of civilization, from the primitive cul-ture to the sophisticated.

"The Shimerdas," the first book of *My Ántonia,* introduces from the start the drama of time in the vivid accounts of the shifting seasons. The book encompasses one year, beginning with the arrival in autumn of the Shimerdas and Jim Burden on the endless Nebraska prairie, portraying the terrible struggle for mere existence in the bleakness of the plains' win-ter, dramatizing the return of life with the arrival of spring, and conclud-ing with the promise of rich harvest in the intense heat of the prairie's summer. This is Jim Burden's remembered year, and it is his obsession with the cycle of time that has caused him to recall Ántonia in a setting of the changing seasons.

Almost every detail in "The Shimerdas" is calculated to shrink the significance of the human drama in contrast with the drama of the seasons, the drama of nature, the drama of the land and sky. The struggle becomes, then, not merely a struggle for a minimum subsistence from the stubborn, foreign soil, but also even more a struggle to re-create and assert existence in a seemingly hostile or indifferent land. No doubt all of the Nebraska pioneers experienced Jim Burden's sensation on arriving on the prairie: "Between that earth and that sky I felt erased, blotted out."

The drama of "The Shimerdas" is the drama of the human being at the mercy of the cyclic nature of the universe. The "glorious autumn" of their arrival on the treeless prairie contributes to that acute sense that "the world was left behind" and that they "had got over the edge of it." The autumn is not the autumn of bountiful nature but the autumn of vast dis-tances and approaching death. The descent of the winter snows heightens the vast primitive beauty of the undisturbed plains: "The sky was bril-liantly blue, and the sunlight on the glittering white stretches of prairie was almost blinding." But even innate to the sharp-colored beauty is an apparent hostility. The whiteness not only blinds but brings in its wake despair and death. When, after the first primitive struggle is over, Ántonia cries out to Jim in the midst of summer, "I wish my papa live to see this summer. I wish no winter ever come again," she displays intuitive insight into the relation of her father's suicide to the cosmic order of time which decrees that the death of winter must unfailingly follow the ripening autumn.

Like autumn, spring when it comes to the prairie is not so much manifest in visible nature as it is a hovering presence compellingly alive and dominant: "There was only—spring itself; the throb of it, the light restlessness, the vital essence of it everywhere: in the sky, in the swift clouds, in the pale sunshine, and in the warm, high wind." It is only with the arrival of spring, at its appointed time, that the Shimerdas and the Burdens, Ántonia and Jim, can emerge from the enforced retreat of winter to look forward to some benevolence from the enduring land. But as the winter shaped, and even took, the life of the prairie pioneer, so the spring imposes a cruelly exacting ritual of tilling and tending the virgin land. Life is hard and the soil close and unyielding without its due. And the "breathless, brilliant heat" of summer, when it descends with fiery fury on the empty lands, brings with its devastation also fertility: "The burning sun of those few weeks, with occasional rains at night, secured the corn."

Throughout the first book of *My Ántonia,* it is the world of nature rather than the human world which dominates, and even the human beings tend to identify themselves with the things of the land. One of Jim Burden's first vivid sensations in the new land is in his grandmother's garden: "I was something that lay under the sun and felt it, like the pumpkins, and I did not want to be anything more. I was entirely happy." During their first year on the prairie the rotation of the decreed seasons imposes a primitive existence not far different from that of the plains' animals, and impresses on the pioneers a keenly felt truth: "In a new country a body feels friendly to the animals." If in the garden Jim imagined himself a pumpkin, there were other times when he and the rest felt a sympathetic resemblance to the gopher, in their intimate dependence on the land for sustenance and home. At the end of this first year's struggle with the land, Ántonia emerges with an essential and profound wisdom that only the cyclic seasons in their cruelty and their beneficence could bestow. She reveals to Jim, "Things . . . will be hard for us."

As Ántonia and Jim are shaped and "created" by the successive seasons, so their lives in turn are cycles of a larger order in time, and shape and create the nation. It is in the dramatization of Ántonia from the girl-hood of the opening pages through her physical flowering in the middle books to, finally, her reproduction of the race in a flock of fine boys in the final pages of the book that her life is represented, like the year with its seasons, as a cycle complete in its stages of birth, growth, fruition and de-cline. Although Ántonia's life represents a greater cycle than that of the year, the pattern remains the same in both. The year, of course, is merely a term for the designation of a unit of time, and its resemblance to the life-cycle suggests that life, too, is a physical representation of time.

As the seasons of fall, winter, spring and summer impose a structure on the first book of Willa Cather's novel, the successive stages of Án-tonia's life assist in imposing a structure on the total work. We may trace these stages through the various books into which the novel is subdivided. Some critics have called Ántonia an earth goddess. She is a re-creation of an archetypal pattern—woman as the embodiment of self-assured if not self-contained physical fertility which insures the endurance of the race. Ántonia never despairs, not even in the first book of the novel in which the hostility of the first prairie winter deprives her of her father; but throughout she works and lives with an innate dignity which springs from her intuitive knowledge of her appointed function in the continuation of the species. Even in the second book, called "The Hired Girls," Ántonia feels no sense of an enforced inferiority but rather a supreme reliance on the hidden resources bestowed upon her by the hard physical struggles of her past.

As Ántonia stands out sharply in the first book, in the second she merges with many "hired girls" in Black Hawk who are of her kind, and in the third, called "Lena Lingard," she does not even appear except as a remembered presence in the talks about the past between Lena and Jim Burden in Lincoln. In these conversations there is a foreshadowing of Án-tonia's fate which is the subject of the fourth book, entitled "The Pioneer Woman's Story." If in book 1 Ántonia represents the eternal endurance under supreme hardship of woman appointed propagator of the race, and in book 2 she represents the overflowing liveliness and energetic abun-dance of physical woman come to the flower, in books 3 and 4 she sym-bolizes the calm and faithful endurance of woman eternally wronged. In Ántonia's fierce love for her fatherless child exists the full explanation of mankind's continuing to be. But Willa Cather insists on Ántonia's appear-ing in a double role, not only as woman wronged, but also as woman ful-filled in her destiny. In the last book of the novel, "Cuzak's Boys," Án-tonia is glimpsed in her declining years surrounded by the "explosive life" of her many children. When Jim Burden sees her after the absence of all those years, he recognizes in her the persistence of that quality he had sensed when they roamed the prairie as boy and girl: "She was there, in the full vigour of her personality, battered but not diminished, looking at me, speaking to me in the husky, breathy voice I remembered so well."

In the closing books of *My Ántonia* ("The Pioneer Woman's Story" and "Cuzak's Boys"), Ántonia emerges as vividly as she did in the first. For an explanation of the fading of Ántonia in books 2 and 3 ("The Hired Girls" and "Lena Lingard"), we must turn to a third principle of structure operating in the book, another cycle greater in scope than either a year or a life. For a foreshadowing of this cycle we may turn to Frederick Jackson Turner and his famous essay, "The Significance of the Frontier in American History." Turner asserted, in the late nineteenth century, that the distinguishing feature of America's development was the cyclic character of her movement westward, conquering over and over again a new wilderness. There was, Turner said, "a recurrence of the process of evolution in each western area reached in the process of expansion."

My Ántonia exemplifies superbly Turner's concept of the recurring cultural evolution on the frontier. There is first of all the migration from the East, in the case of the Shimerdas from Czechoslovakia, in Jim Burden's case from Virginia, both lands of a high cultural level. In the West these comparatively sophisticated people are compelled literally to begin over again, on a primitive level, shedding their cultural attainment like an animal its skin, and, like animals, doing battle with the land and the elements for the meanest food and shelter.

The books of *My Ántonia* reflect the varying stages of this evolutionary process in cultural development. On this level of structure, not the seasons of the year, nor the phases of Ántonia's life, but the successive cultural plateaus of the nation operate as ordering elements in the novel. And it is on this level of significance and in the dramatization of this epic archetypal cycle of the country that justification for those sections of the book, so frequently condemned because they lose focus on Ántonia, may be found.

In the first book, "The Shimerdas," the newly arrived pioneers from the East discover nothing but their strength and the prairie's stubborn soil out of which to create for themselves a new world in their own image. In this primitive struggle with the prairie, on a level with the struggle of prehistoric man in the dawn of time, some lose their lives, some their spirit, and all lose that overlay of softening civilization which they brought from the East. There is not only the primitive struggle, but these pioneers become primitive men in the harshness of the struggle. Ántonia's father, sad for the old country, dies; and Ántonia takes a man's place behind the plow. On the prairie the elements, the sky and the land impose a communal democracy in all of the meager human institutions.

"The Hired Girls," the second book of *My Ántonia,* portrays a higher stage in the cultural evolution of the frontier: the small town comes to the wilderness. If Jim Burden discovers his own hidden courage and becomes a man in the snake-killing incident of book 1, in book 2 he discovers the genuine complexity of adulthood, especially in a social context which the bare prairie does not afford. Jim is puzzled by the stratification of society in Black Hawk, a stratification that could not exist on the virgin prairie, and which does not tally with Jim's moral judgment: the "hired girls" are for Jim the most interesting, the most exciting and the liveliest of all possible companions, far superior to the dull conformists of the town. It is the strong lure of the hired girls, however, which precipitates Jim's first crucial decision: in spite of the strong spiritual and physical attraction of these girls, Jim turns to the study which will prepare him for college and which, in Black Hawk, culminates in the triumph of his high school commencement oration. Already there has come to the frontier prairie that element whose absence caused Ántonia's father to despair. After Ántonia has heard Jim's speech, she tells him: "there was something in your speech that made me think so about my papa." In her instinctive way Ántonia dimly understands her father's sacrifice of his life and Jim's yearning for higher intellectual achievement, even though her own destiny, centered in the physical reproduction of the race, may be and is to be fulfilled on the innocent and unsophisticated prairie.

Jim's discoveries, both intellectual and emotional, of book 2, are continued and intensified in the next book, "Lena Lingard." Lincoln, Nebraska, is as far above Black Hawk culturally as Black Hawk is above the empty, untouched prairie, and though the university has the limitations imposed by the isolation of the plains, there is "an atmosphere of endeavour, of expectancy and bright hopefulness" which prevails. It is Jim's good fortune to develop a close association with Gaston Cleric, the intellectually alive and intense head of the Latin Department, who introduces Jim to the exciting world of ideas. Jim discovers that "when one first enters that world everything else fades for a time, and all that went before is as if it had not been." But the climax of Jim's awakening is a realization of the persistence of the past: "Yet I found curious survivals; some of the figures of my old life seemed to be waiting for me in the new." Jim's awareness of the crucial impingement of his prairie heritage on his involvement in a received culture seems an instinctive artistic confirmation of Turner's frontier thesis.

Culture does come to the Nebraska prairie, not only in the form of a world of ideas via Gaston Cleric, but also in the form of music and theater. The nature of the curious impact is revealed brilliantly when Jim describes his and Lena's reaction to the traveling "Camille": "A couple of jackrabbits, run in off the prairie, could not have been more innocent of what awaited them." Throughout book 3 of the novel, there is a delightful rediscovery by the children of the pioneer generation of a cultural world forsaken by their parents for the hard and isolated life of the prairie. But the pioneer values of freshness and courage and integrity—and many more—survive and condition the responses.

Lincoln, Nebraska, though it offers much, offers a mere token of what waits in the rich and glittering East. Lured on by bright dreams of intellectual achievement, Jim Burden follows Gaston Cleric to Harvard, which, in the book's developing hierarchy, is to Lincoln as Lincoln is to Black Hawk and Black Hawk to the barren prairie. But with the dramatization of three stages of civilization as it comes to the wilderness, and with the suggestion of the future destiny by the "invocation" of "ancient" Harvard and by the suggestion of greater cultural riches farther East, Willa Cather shifts the focus from the dream of the nation and, indeed, of civilization, back to Ántonia of the prairies. The novel has, in a sense, come full circle when Jim, in the last book, finds himself in the midst of that very culture the nostalgic remembrance of which drove Ántonia's father to despair: "Once when I was abroad I went into Bohemia, and from Prague I sent Ántonia some photographs of her native village." By this casual visit, the return to the point of origin, the cycle of cultural movement is symbolically completed. And when the sophisticated, world-traveled, perhaps even world-weary, Jim Burden returns to the prairie scenes of his boyhood and discovers Ántonia and her houseful of boys, he discovers at the same time the enduring quality of those values not dependent on cultural level, but accessible on the untutored prairies. Ántonia, "in the full vigour of her personality, battered but not diminished," not only endures but achieves an emotionally and physically fulfilled life. Her boys are her triumphant creative achievement.

My Ántonia closes with the dominant image of the circle, a significant reminder of the general movement of all the structural elements in the book. After his visit with Ántonia, Jim confesses, "I had the sense of coming home to myself, and of having found out what a little circle man's experience is." This vivid image reinforces the cyclic theme which pervades the book: the cycle of the seasons of the year, the cycle of the stages of human life, the cycle of the cultural phases of civilization. *My Ántonia* is then, ultimately about time, about the inexorable movement of future into present, of present into past. Against the backdrop of this epic drama of the repetitive movement of time, man poignantly plays out his role. Ántonia, when she cries out to Jim, "I wish no winter ever come again," more nearly expresses the essence of the book's theme than does Jim when he asserts at the end, "whatever we had missed, we possessed together the precious, the incommunicable past." *Optima dies . . . prima fugit,* translated by Jim as "the best days are the first to flee," stands as the book's epigraph. This intensely felt awareness of the past *as past* is the emotional heart of the novel, and is evoked and sustained by the book's several levels of structure and their involvement with the revolving cycles of time.

Hope and Memory in *My Ántonia*

Robert E. Scholes

R. W. B. Lewis in *The American Adam* has suggested that the "most fruit-ful" ideas circulating in nineteenth-century America were embodied in the image of "the authentic American as a figure of heroic innocence and vast potentialities, poised at the start of a new history." The currency of this image, according to Mr. Lewis, dates from the close of the War of 1812, and is prominent in the writings of both philosophers and journalists in pre-Civil War America. Mr. Lewis is relatively successful in demonstrat-ing that men like Emerson, Thoreau, Holmes, Lowell and the elder Henry James were concerned with this vision of the new American man; but he is much less convincing when he attempts to show that their novelist con-temporaries relied on this same notion in their works. He is put to such shifts as considering the *last* novel of Hawthorne and of Melville, rather than their *best* in his attempt to illustrate the ubiquity of the Adamic idea.

The great fruition in fiction of the theme of the heroic innocent in conflict with society actually occurred in the latter part of the nineteenth century and the early part of the twentieth. Whether this theme was really important in the works of Melville and Hawthorne, and whether novelists will find it stimulating or useful in the future are two questions beyond the scope of the present inquiry (though I suspect the answer to both should be negative). It is nevertheless interesting to note that the American Innocent was a major preoccupation of American novelists from James and Howells down to Willa Cather and F. Scott Fitzgerald. And it may be use-

From *Shenandoah* 14, no. 1 (Autumn 1962). © 1962 by Washington and Lee Uni-versity.

ful to examine exactly how one novelist, Willa Cather, made use of the Adamic myth in her fullest treatment of it: *My Ántonia*.

As Mr. Lewis distills it, the myth of Adam in America is that of an "individual emancipated from history, happily bereft of ancestry, untouched and undefiled by the usual inheritances of family and race; an individual standing alone, self-propelling, ready to confront whatever awaited him with the aid of his own unique and inherent resources." This Adamic person is "thrust into an actual world and an actual age," and, in the fully developed myth, undergoes a "fall": suffers "the necessary transforming shocks and sufferings, the experiments and errors . . . through which maturity and identity may be arrived at." Mr. Lewis is a bit mysterious about what he means by "identity," but self-knowledge or self-discovery are probably safe, if not totally accurate substitutes.

The two central figures in *My Ántonia* are, in different senses, Innocents. Jim Burden, bereft of both his parents within a year, is removed from the warm and comfortable Virginia of his early days and thrust into the strange and frightening world of Nebraska. As he bumps along on the wagon ride to his new home, he feels that he has left even the spirits of his dead parents behind him:

> The wagon jolted on, carrying me I know not whither. I don't think I was homesick. If we never arrived anywhere, it did not matter. Between that earth and that sky I felt erased, blotted out. I did not say my prayers that night: here, I felt, what would be would be.

Ántonia Shimerda, though also a young, innocent creature in a raw country, is not bereft of the past as Jim Burden is. Ántonia's Bohemian ancestry is a part of her and exerts a decided influence on her present and future. We are reminded of this past constantly: by the Bohemian customs and culinary practices of the Shimerdas; by the observations of Otto Fuchs on the relationship of Austrians and Bohemians in the old country; and especially by the Catholic religion of the Bohemians, which is their strongest link with the past, and which serves to bind them together and to separate them from the Protestant society of their adopted land. But, most important, Ántonia herself cherishes her connection with the past. When Jim asks if she remembers the little town of her birth, she replies,

> "Jim . . . if I was put down there in the middle of the night, I could find my way all over that little town; and along the river where my grandmother lived. My feet remember all the little paths through the woods, and where the big roots stick out to trip you. I ain't never forgot my own country."

But despite the importance of the past for Ántonia, she and the other hired girls are figures of heroic and vital innocence, associated with nature and the soil. Like Lena Lingard, they all "waked fresh with the world every day." They are unused to the ways of society, and Ántonia, especially, is too trusting. Lena tells Jim that Ántonia "won't hear a word against [Larry Donovan]. She's so sort of innocent." The struggle of the "hired girls" with society is one of the important themes of the novel. Jim Burden remarks that

> the country girls were considered a menace to the social order. Their beauty shone out too boldly against a conventional background. But anxious mothers need have felt no alarm. They mistook the mettle of their sons. The respect for respectability was stronger than any desire in Black Hawk youth.

This struggle of the country girls with the city is a very perplexing one, in which apparent victory and apparent defeat are both apt to prove evanescent in time. Lena Lingard and Tiny Soderball become successful, triumphing even in the metropolis of San Francisco, while Ántonia becomes the foolish victim of her love for a conniving railroad conductor. But Lena and Tiny succeed only in becoming more like the society from which they had been ostracized, while Ántonia, and the other country girls who stay on the land, ultimately change the structure of society itself. Jim Burden remarks,

> I always knew I should live long enough to see my country girls come into their own, and I have. Today the best that a harassed Black Hawk merchant can hope for is to sell provisions and farm machinery and automobiles to the rich farms where that first crop of stalwart Bohemian and Scandinavian girls are now the mistresses.

Jim Burden, like Lena and Tiny, has made his success in the city and on the city's terms. From the narrator of the introductory chapter we learn that Jim's personal life, his marriage, has not been a success though his legal work flourishes. Jim's failure to find happiness or satisfaction in his career and in the city, constitutes for him the "fall" into self-knowledge which is characteristic of the Adamic hero. It is Jim's recognition of his own fall that makes him superior to Lena and Tiny, and enables him to live vicariously through Ántonia and her children.

Ántonia's seduction is a more clear-cut "fall" than Jim's unhappiness, and her subsequent self-knowledge is more strikingly evidenced. When Jim meets Ántonia after she has had her illegitimate child, he notices "a new kind of strength in the gravity of her face." At this meeting she asks Jim whether he has learned to like big cities, adding that she would die of lonesomeness in such a place. "I like to be where I know every stack and tree, and where all the ground is friendly," she says; and after they part Jim feels "the old pull of the earth, the solemn magic that comes out of those fields at night-fall," and he wishes he could be a little boy again, and that his way would end there.

When Jim revisits Ántonia and her thriving family, she has in some ways relapsed toward the past. " 'I've forgot my English so.' " She says, " 'I don't often talk it any more. I tell the children I used to speak it real well.' She said they all spoke Bohemian at home. The little ones could not speak English at all—didn't learn it until they went to school." But her children, her involvement in life, make her concerned for the future. She has lived "much and hard," reflects Jim as they meet, but "she was there in the full vigor of her personality, battered but not diminished, looking at me, speaking to me in the husky, breathy voice I remembered so well." Jim, however, is not recognized by Ántonia at first, even though he has "kept so young." He is less battered, perhaps, but he is more diminished.

So it is that Ántonia, who is always conscious of the past, is nevertheless free of it, and capable of concern for the future. And her past is not merely that of a generation or so. Jim observes, "She lent herself to immemorial human attitudes which we recognize by instinct as universal and true. . . . It was no wonder that her sons stood tall and straight. She was a rich mine of life, like the founders of early races." Whereas Jim, who has no such connection with the past, who came to Nebraska without a family and rode on a wagon into a new life which he felt was beyond even the attention of God, is still bound by the recent past, by what has happened to him in his own youth, and he lives in both the present and the future only vicariously through the plans and lives of others. He reflects, "In the course of twenty crowded years one parts with many illusions. I did not wish to lose the early ones. Some memories are realities, and are better than anything that can happen to one again." Jim is haunted by the past, by the sense that, in the phrase of Virgil which is the novel's epigraph, *Optima dies . . . prima fugit.* When he contemplates in the closing lines of his narrative the road on which he had entered his new life as a boy, he reconsiders his whole existence:

> I had the sense of coming home to myself, and of having found out what a little circle man's experience is. For Ántonia and for me, this had been the road of Destiny; had taken us to those

early accidents of fortune which predetermined for us all that we can ever be. Now I understood that the same road was to bring us together again. Whatever we had missed, we possessed together the precious, the incommunicable past.

Ántonia's life is not tragic. She is neither defeated nor destroyed by life, not even diminished. Yet the distinguishing characteristic of this novel is its elegiac tone; the eternal note of sadness pervades especially the closing passages of the book. The direct cause of this element of sadness is the nostalgia of Jim Burden, through which the story of Ántonia filters down to the reader. But behind Jim Burden's nostalgia, and merged with it, is the nostalgia of Willa Cather herself.

There is a suggestion in this novel and in the earlier *O Pioneers!* that the younger brothers and the sisters of this splendid generation of pioneer women will not be their equals. Emil Bergson—the youth in *O Pioneers!* for whom his older sister Alexandra labors and plans—attends the university, escapes from the plough, only to ruin several lives through his adulterous love. And in *My Ántonia* there is the suggestion that the coming generations will be less heroic and more ordinary than the present breed. Jim Burden at one point muses on this problem, thinking of the hired girls in Black Hawk:

> Those girls had grown up in the first bitter-hard times, and had got little schooling themselves. But the younger brothers and sisters, for whom they made such sacrifices and who have had "advantages," never seem to me, when I meet them now, half as interesting or as well educated. The older girls, who helped to break up the wild sod, learned so much from life, from poverty, from their mothers and grandmothers; they had all, like Ántonia, been early awakened and made observant by coming at a tender age from an old country to a new.

The circumstances which formed Ántonia will not be repeated; the future will be in the hands of a diminished race. It is the feeling which haunts Willa Cather's novel. Ántonia looks to the future of her children, but Jim Burden knows that the future will be at best a poor imitation of the past. Ántonia's life is a triumph of innocence and vitality over hardship and evil. But Willa Cather does not celebrate this triumph; rather, she intones an elegy over the dying myth of the heroic Innocent, over the days that are no more.

Willa Cather

Dorothy Van Ghent

In Willa Cather's . . . *My Ántonia* (1918), there occurs a majestic, mysterious image that suggests . . . the timeless aspect of the subject matter which seems most naturally her own. Jim Burden (the narrator of the story) and some "hired girls" from the little Nebraska town of Black Hawk have spent a lazy afternoon by the river, ending with a picnic supper.

> Presently we saw a curious thing: There were no clouds, the sun was going down in a limpid, gold-washed sky. Just as the lower edge of the red disk rested on the high fields against the horizon, a great black figure suddenly appeared on the face of the sun. We sprang to our feet, straining our eyes toward it. In a moment we realized what it was. On some upland farm, a plough had been left standing in the field. The sun was sinking just behind it. Magnified across the distance by the horizontal light, it stood out against the sun, was exactly contained within the circle of the disk; the handles, the tongue, the share—black against the molten red. There it was, heroic in size, a picture writing on the sun. Even while we whispered about it, our vision disappeared; the ball dropped and dropped until the red tip went beneath the earth. The fields below us were dark, the sky was growing pale, and that forgotten plough had sunk back to its own littleness somewhere on the prairie.

From *Willa Cather: Pamphlets of American Writers*, no. 36. © 1964 by the University of Minnesota. University of Minnesota Press, 1964.

The image could have been carved, as a sacred life-symbol, on the stones of a lost temple of Yucatan, or in a tomb of the Valley of Kings. The plow itself, forgotten on that upland farm, could have been left there by some farmer of Chaldea.

The story is as much Jim Burden's as it is Ántonia's. The two children share the initiatory experiences of the wild land to which their parents have brought them. Jim's family, like Willa Cather's, are from Virginia; Ántonia Shimerda's family are Bohemians who have come to take up homestead rights in the new country. Jim's family live in a house, Ántonia's in a cave in a clay bank, the children sleeping in holes tunneled into the gumbo mud. Around them is "nothing but land: not a country at all, but the material out of which countries are made." It is like the sea, featureless and barren, but running with obscure, unaccountable movement as of the rushing of theromorphic gods: "I felt that the grass was the country, as the water is the sea. The red of the grass made all the great prairie the colour . . . of certain seaweeds when they are first washed up. And there was so much motion in it; the whole country seemed, somehow, to be running . . . as if the shaggy grass were a sort of loose hide, and underneath it herds of wild buffalo were galloping, galloping." The ends of the earth are very near. "The light air about me told me that the world ended here": one had only to walk straight on through the red grass to the edge of the world where there would be only sun and sky left.

Out of homely American detail are composed certain friezelike entablatures that have the character of ancient ritual and sculpture. There is the suicide and funeral of Mr. Shimerda, Ántonia's father, a gifted musician who could, finally, not bear the animal life to which the first generation of pioneers were subjected. For his suicide he dressed himself fastidiously in the fine clothes of the concert hall, went out to the cow barn, and shot himself. It was dead winter, and his corpse had got frozen to the ground before it was discovered. It was left there safely till the day of the funeral, when the hired men from the Burden farm "went ahead on horseback to cut the body loose from the pool of blood in which it was frozen fast to the ground." The Shimerdas were Roman Catholic, an anomaly in that predominantly Protestant neighborhood of farmers, and as a suicide he could not be buried in Catholic ground, so his grave was made at a crossroads in the age-old superstition clinging to the suicide. But no roads ever crossed over his grave. "The road from the north curved a little to the east just there, and the road from the west swung out a little to the south; so that the grave, with its tall red grass that was never mowed, was like a little island." And Jim Burden says, "I loved the dim superstition, the propitiatory intent, that had put the grave there; and still more I loved the spirit that could not carry out the sentence—the error from the surveyed lines, the clemency of the soft earth roads along which the home-coming wagons rattled after sunset."

There are the hired men on the farm, Jake and Otto, who, with the "sag of their tired shoulders against the whitewashed wall," form a mute memorial as dignified and tender in outline as a Greek stele—nomadic figures who bear with them the ancient pathos of mysterious coming and mysterious departure, "without warning . . . on the westbound train one morning, in their Sunday clothes, with their oilcloth valises—and I never saw them again." And there are the hired girls, girls who like Ántonia came from the farming community to take domestic work in the town of Black Hawk; robust, exuberant, and held in contempt by the townspeople, these girls appear like a sunlit band of caryatids, or like the succession of peasant girls who loved generously and suffered tragically in old ballads, or like the gay interlinked chain of girls in Proust's *Á l'ombre des jeunes filles en fleurs*. "When I closed my eyes," Jim Burden says, "I could hear them all laughing—the Danish laundry girls and the three Bohemian Marys. . . . It came over me, as it had never done before, the relation between girls like those and the poetry of Virgil. If there were no girls like them in the world, there would be no poetry. I understood that clearly, for the first time."

Jim Burden, who goes away to the city and returns to the Nebraska farmland only after long intervals, is able to register that Chekhovian "suffering of change" which enters Willa Cather's work during this period. On his last return both he and Ántonia are middle-aged, Jim a weary intellectual nomad, Ántonia married to a Bohemian farmer with a brood of children about her, gay in her orchards and her kitchen. With scarcely a tooth in her head, save for some broken brown snags, she is still able to leave "images in the mind that did not fade—that grew stronger with time . . . She lent herself to immemorial human attitudes which we recognize by instinct as universal and true." The suffering of change, the sense of irreparable loss in time, is one polarity of the work; the other polarity is the timelessness of those images associated with Ántonia, with the grave of the suicide at the crossroads, with the mute fortitude of the hired men and the pastoral poetry of the hired girls, and most of all with the earth itself, carrying in mysterious stroke, like the plow hieroglyphed on the sun, signs of an original and ultimate relationship between man and cosmos.

Willa Cather, *My Ántonia*

Wallace Stegner

If, as is often said, every novelist is born to write one thing, then the one thing that Willa Cather was born to write was first fully realized in *My Ántonia* (1918). In that novel the people are the Bohemian and Swedish immigrants she had known in her childhood on the Nebraska plains; the prose is the prose of her maturity—flexible, evocative, already tending to a fastidious bareness but not yet gone pale and cool; the novelistic skill is of the highest, the structure at once free and intricately articulated; the characters stretch into symbolic suggestiveness as naturally as trees cast shadows in the long light of a prairie evening; the theme is the fully exposed, complexly understood theme of the American orphan or exile, struggling to find a place between an Old World left behind and a New World not yet created.

But to say that Willa Cather found her subject and her manner and her theme in *My Ántonia* is not to say that she found them easily. When *My Ántonia* appeared, Miss Cather was forty-five years old. She had already had one career as a teacher and another as an editor, and she had published a good many short stories and three other novels.

The first of these, *Alexander's Bridge* (1912), was a nearly total mistake—a novel laid in London and dealing with the attenuated characters and fragile ethical problems of the genteel tradition. In writing it, Miss Cather later remarked, she was trying to sing a song that did not lie in her voice. Urged by her friend Sarah Orne Jewett to try something closer to

From *The American Novel from James Fenimore Cooper to William Faulkner,* edited by Wallace Stegner. © 1965 by Basic Books, Inc.

her own experience, she revived her Western memories with a trip to Arizona and New Mexico and, after her return to Pittsburgh,

> began to write a story entirely for myself; a story about some Scandinavians and Bohemians who had been neighbours of ours when I lived on a ranch in Nebraska, when I was eight or nine years old. I found it a much more absorbing occupation than writing *Alexander's Bridge;* a different process altogether. Here there was no arranging or "inventing"; everything was spontaneous and took its own place. . . . This was like taking a ride through familiar country on a horse that knew the way, on a fine morning when you felt like riding.

As she herself instantly recognized, that second book, *O Pioneers!* (1913), came close to being the tune that "lay in her voice." She wrote it spontaneously because she was tapping both memory and affection. She thought of the subject matter as a considerable innovation, because no American writer had yet used Swedish immigrants for any but comic purposes, and nobody had ever written about Nebraska, considered in literary circles the absolute home of the clodhopper. Actually, there was nothing so revolutionary about the subject matter—it was merely one further extension of the local-color curiosity about little-known places and picturesque local types. Hamlin Garland had done German and Norwegian immigrants very like these, on Wisconsin and Iowa farms very like Miss Cather's Nebraska ones, in *Main-Travelled Roads* (1891). *O Pioneers!* was new in its particulars, but not new in type, and it was not Willa Cather's fully trained voice that was heard in it. In its method, the book is orthodox; the heroine, Alexandra Bergson, is a type of earth goddess; the theme is the theme of the conquest of a hard country that had dominated novels of the American settlement ever since James Fenimore Cooper's *The Pioneers* in 1823. Miss Cather's novel, in fact, is considerably slighter and simpler than Cooper's of similar title.

In her third book, *The Song of the Lark* (1915), we can see Miss Cather systematically and consciously working for the enlargement and complication of her theme. The locale, at least in the beginning, is again Nebraska, though she calls it Colorado; the chief character is again a local girl of immigrant parentage, great promise, and few advantages. But the antagonist here is not the earth, and triumph is nothing so simple as the hewing of a farm out of a hard country. To the problem of survival has been added the problem of culture. The struggle is involved with the training of Thea Kronborg's fine voice; the effort of the novel is to explore how a talent may find expression even when it appears in a crude little railroad town on the plains, and how a frontier American may lift himself from his traditionless, artless environment to full stature as an artist and an individual.

Here we see developing the dynamism between Old World and New that occurs strongly again not only in *My Ántonia* but in *One of Ours* (1922), *The Professor's House* (1925), *Death Comes for the Archbishop* (1927), *Shadows on the Rock* (1931), and several of the short stories such as "Neighbor Rosicky." It is as if Miss Cather conceived the settlement of her country as a marriage between a simple, fresh, hopeful young girl and a charming, worldly, but older man. Thea Kronborg's German music teacher, Herr Wunsch, is the first of those cultivated and unhappy Europeans who people Miss Cather's fictions—exiles who, though doomed themselves by the hardships of pioneering, pass on sources of life and art to the eager young of a new land. Thea, like Alexandra Bergson before her and Ántonia Shimerda later, is that best sort of second generation American who learns or retains some of the intellectual and artistic tradition of Europe without losing the American freshness and without falling into the common trap of a commercial and limited "practicality." These are all success stories of sorts, and all reflect a very American groping toward a secure identity.

But even *The Song of the Lark* was not the precise song that lay in Willa Cather's voice. Or rather, it was the right tune, but she sang it imperfectly. The story of Thea Kronborg's struggle to become an opera singer is told with a realism so detailed that it is exhausting; and it ended by offending its author nearly as much as the pretentiousness of *Alexander's Bridge*. "Too much detail," she concluded later, "is apt, like any form of extravagance, to become slightly vulgar." She never tried a second time the "full-blooded method": When the next book came along, "quite of itself, and with no direction from me, it took the road of O Pioneers!—not the road of *The Song of the Lark*."

The next one was, of course, *My Ántonia*. But the road it took was not quite exactly that of *O Pioneers!* For though the place is still Nebraska and the protagonist is still an immigrant girl contending with the handicaps of a physical and emotional transplanting, *My Ántonia* is a major novel where the earlier ones were trial efforts. *O Pioneers!* was truly simple; *My Ántonia* only looks simple. *The Song of the Lark* was cluttered in its attempt to deal with complexity; *My Ántonia* gives complexity the clean lines and suggestive subtlety of fine architecture.

One technical device which is fundamental to the greater concentration and suggestiveness of *My Ántonia* is the point of view from which it is told. Both of the earlier "Nebraska novels" had been reported over the protagonist's shoulder, with omniscient intrusions by the author. Here the whole story is told by a narrator, Jim Burden, a boyhood friend of Ántonia, later a lawyer representing the railroads. The use of the narrative mask permits Miss Cather to exercise her sensibility without obvious self-indulgence: Burden becomes an instrument of the selectivity that she worked for. He also permits the easy condensation and syncopation of time—an indispensable technical tool in a novel that covers more than thirty years and deals in a complex way with a theme of development. Finally, Jim Burden is used constantly as a suggestive parallel to Ántonia: he is himself an orphan and has been himself transplanted (from the East, from Virginia), and is himself groping for an identity and an affiliation. In the process of understanding and commemorating Ántonia, he locates himself; we see the essential theme from two points, and the space between those points serves as a base line for triangulation.

The parallel is stressed from the beginning, when Jim, an orphan of ten, arrives in Black Hawk, Nebraska, on his way to live with his grandparents, and sees the immigrant Shimerda family huddling in bewilderment on the station platform, speaking their strange lost tongue. As he is driven to the ranch under a great unfamiliar sky, across a land that planes off mysteriously into darkness—"not a country, but the material out of which countries are made"—Jim feels so lost and strange and uprooted that he cannot even say the prayers that have been taught him back in Virginia. "Between that earth and sky I felt erased, blotted out."

For Jim, protected by his relatives, the strangeness soon wears away. For the Shimerdas, who have none of the tools or skills of farmers, no friends, no English, and who discover that the land they have been sold is bad and their house a sod cave, transplanting is a harsher trial, and harder on the old than on the young, and on the sensitive than on the dull. With the help of their neighbors the Burdens, the Shimerdas make a beginning, but before their first Christmas in the new land Papa Shimerda, gentle, helpless, homesick for the old life in Prague, has killed himself with a shotgun. Survival, which Miss Cather presents as a process of inevitable brutalization, is best managed by the grasping Mama Shimerda and her sullen son Ambrosch. The fourteen-year-old girl, Ántonia, pretty and intelligent and her father's darling, must put off any hope of schooling and become one of the breadwinners for her miserably poor family. The deprivation is symbolic: this is the deculturation enforced on the frontier. The one thing beautiful in her life, the thing she shares with Jim, is the land itself, the great sea of grass, the wild roses in the fence corners of spring, the mighty weathers, and the tiny things—insects and flowers and little animals—that the eye notices because on the plains there is so little else to take the attention.

Ántonia and Jim as children share a kind of Eden, but they are going toward different futures. At the end of the first long section, which is divided between the presentation of the hardships of an immigrant family and Miss Cather's delicate nostalgic evocation of the freedom and beauty of the untamed land, Jim and Ántonia are lying together on top of the Burdens' chicken house while a great electrical storm comes on and "the felty beat of raindrops" begins in the dust. Why, Jim asks her, can't she always be "nice, like this"? Why must she all the time try to be like her brother Ambrosch? "If I live here like you," Ántonia says, "that is different. Things will be easy for you. But they will be hard for us."

There are gradations in the penalties of exile; the most violently uprooted have the least chance. Book 2 of the novel reinforces this idea by moving the action from the half-idyllic country to the limited and restricting little town of Black Hawk. In pages that forecast some of the attitudes of Sinclair Lewis' *Main Street* (1920), Miss Cather reveals the pettiness and snobbery, the vulgar commercialism, the cultural starvation, the forming class distinctions, the pathetic pleasures of a typical prairie town just beyond the pioneering stage. Ántonia, Lena Lingard, Tiny Soderball, and other Bohemian, Norwegian, and Swedish immigrant girls work as servants in the houses of the so-called "better families," and though they are snubbed by the town girls they demonstrate in their vitality and health something sturdier and more admirable than the more advantaged can show. Those for whom "things are easy" develop less character than these girls deprived of school, forced to work at menial jobs, dedicating their wages to help their families back on the farm. They do not even know that Black Hawk is a deprived little hole, but throw themselves wholeheartedly into the town dances and into any pleasure and excitement their world affords. Miss Cather sums up both desire and deprivation in a brief winter scene:

> In the winter bleakness a hunger for colour came over people, like the Laplander's craving for fats and sugar. Without knowing why, we used to linger on the sidewalk outside the church when the lamps were lighted early for choir practice or prayer-meeting, shivering and talking until our feet were like lumps of ice. The crude reds and greens and blues of that coloured glass held us there.

It is Jim Burden speaking, but he speaks even more for the "hired girls" than for himself, for he is not confined within Black Hawk's limitations as they are. For him there is more than crude colored glass; opportunity opens outward to the state university in the city of Lincoln. For Ántonia and the others there is only housework, the amorous advances of people like Wick Cutter, the town moneylender, and the probability that eventually they will marry some farmer of their own immigrant background, who will work them like farm horses.

Book 3 of *My Ántonia* has been objected to as a structural mistake, because it turns away from Ántonia and focuses on the university and city life of Jim Burden—on the opening of his mind, the passionate response he makes to books and ideas under the tutelage of a favorite professor, the quiet affair he has with Lena Lingard, who has set up in the city as a dressmaker. But the criticism seems based on too simplistic a view of the novel's intention. Though the title suggests that Ántonia is the focus of the book, the development from the symbolic beginning scene is traced through both Ántonia and Jim, and a good part of that theme of development is concerned with the possible responses to deprivation and to opportunity. We leave Ántonia in book 3 in order to return to her with more understanding later.

A high point of Jim's life in Lincoln is a performance of *Camille* that he and Lena Lingard attend. Like so many of Miss Cather's scenes, it expands effortlessly out of the particular and into the symbolic. The performance is shabby, the actors are broken-down, but to Jim the play is magic. Its bright illusion concentrates for him everything that he hopes for as he starts east to Harvard to continue his studies, going farther from his country, back toward the intellectual and artistic things that his country has left behind or possesses only in second-rate and vulgarized forms. It is worth observing that Jim Burden leaves Nebraska on a note of illusion.

Book 4 returns us to Ántonia and to Black Hawk. Back after two years at Harvard, Jim hears that in his absence Ántonia has eloped with a railroad conductor and that after being deceived and abandoned she has returned to her brother Ambrosch's farm to bear her child and work in the fields like a man. The contrast between her pitiful failure and Jim's growing opportunities is deliberate; so is the trick of letting Jim come back to Ántonia little by little, first through the stories told of her by townspeople and only later in person. When he does finally go to the farm to see her, the deliberate structural split that began with book 3 is finally mended. Their lives will continue to run in different channels, but they have rediscovered the "old times" that they have in common, the things that by now Ántonia could not bear to leave. "I like to be where I know every stack and tree, and where all the ground is friendly," she says. Her bond is with the land—she all but *is* the land—while Jim will go on to law school and to occupations and associations unimaginable to her. Again Miss Cather catches a significant moment in a reverberating image, to show both the difference and the intimate relationship between these two:

> As we walked homeward across the fields, the sun dropped and lay like a great golden globe in the low west. While it hung there, the moon rose in the east, as big as a cart-wheel, pale silver and streaked with rose colour, thin as a bubble or a ghost-moon. For five, perhaps ten minutes, the two luminaries confronted each other across the level land, resting on opposite edges of the world.

"I'll come back," Jim says, leaving Ántonia, and she replies, "Perhaps you will. But even if you don't, you're here, like my father." Because we must give scenes like these more than realistic value, we recognize here an insistence, not only on the shared beauty of childhood in the new land, but on the other tradition that is going to go on operating in Ántonia's life, the gift of her father with his gentleness and his taste. In Ántonia, New World and Old World, nature and nurture, meet as they meet in Jim, in different proportions and with different emphasis.

That union of two worlds is made explicit in book 5, when twenty years later Jim Burden returns again to Nebraska and finds Ántonia married to an amiable, half-successful Bohemian farmer, with a brood of healthy boys. She is no longer an eager girl, but a worn woman. But the same warmth of spirit still glows in her, and her life that had been half-wrecked has been put back together. In most ways, hers is an American family; but within the family they speak only Czech, and thus something of Papa Shimerda, something of Bohemia, is kept—something related to those strangenesses that Jim Burden had noted as a small boy: the dry brown chips he saw the Shimerdas nibbling, that were dried mushrooms picked in some far-off Bohemian forest; and the way Mama Shimerda, given title to a cow by Jim's grandfather, seized his hand in a totally un–American gesture and kissed it. A partly remembered but valued tradition and an empty land have fused and begun to be something new.

As for Jim Burden, we understand at last that the name Willa Cather chose for him was not picked by accident. For Jim not only, as narrator, carries the "burden" or tune of the novel; he carries also the cultural burden that Willa Cather herself carried, the quintessentially American burden of remaking in the terms of a new place everything that makes life graceful and civilized. To become a European or an easterner is only to reverse and double the exile. The education that lured Jim Burden away from Nebraska had divided him against himself, as Willa Cather was divided. Like people, the education that comes from elsewhere must be modified to fit a new environment. In becoming a man of the world, Jim Burden discovers that he has almost forgotten to be a man from Nebraska. It is Ántonia, who now achieves some of the quality of earth goddess that Alexandra Bergson had in *O Pioneers!*, who reminds him that no matter where his mind has been, his heart has always been here.

Jim Burden at the end of the novel is in the same position that Willa Cather was in when she finally found the people and themes and country that she was "born to write." The final paragraph is like the closing of a door, shutting in things that until now have been exposed or scattered. As Jim walks through the country he stumbles upon a stretch of the old pioneer wagon road of his childhood:

> This was the road over which Ántonia and I came on the night when we got off the train at Black Hawk and were bedded down in the straw, wondering children, being taken we knew not whither. I had only to close my eyes to hear the rumbling of the wagons in the dark, and to be again overcome by that obliterating strangeness. The feelings of that night were so near that I could reach out and touch them with my hand. I had the sense of coming home to myself, and of having found out what a little circle man's experience is. For Ántonia and for me, this had been the road of Destiny; had taken us to those early accidents of fortune which predetermined for us all that we can ever be. Now I understand that the same road was to bring us together again. Whatever we had missed, we possessed together the precious, the incommunicable past.

It is difficult not to hear in that passage the voice of Willa Cather, who like Jim left raw Nebraska to become a citizen of the world, and like him was drawn back. Jim Burden is more than a narrative device: he is an essential part of the theme, a demonstration of how such an American may reconcile the two halves of himself. And Ántonia is more than a woman and a character. Jim describes her toward the end as "a rich mine of life, like the founders of early races." Miss Cather, who did not believe in laboring a point any more than she believed in overfurnishing a novel, clearly wanted us to take away that image of Ántonia. A mine of life, the mother of races, a new thing forming itself in hardship and hope, but clinging to fragments of the well-loved old. Hence *My Ántonia*—any American's Ántonia, Willa Cather's Ántonia. No writer ever posed that essential aspect of the American experience more warmly, with more nostalgic lyricism, or with a surer understanding of what it means.

The Drama of Memory in *My Ántonia*

Terence Martin

In Willa Cather's novels of the West, the land, raw and unsubdued, stands out as the initial force to be confronted. "The great fact was the land itself," she says in describing the milieu of *O Pioneers!* (1913), "which seemed to overwhelm the little beginnings of human society that struggled in its sombre wastes." The far different world of *Death Comes for the Archbishop* (1927), with its vast distances and arid wastes, seems older, earlier, yet equally a "great fact" as Miss Cather emphasizes its primeval quality: the mesa, she writes, "had an appearance of great antiquity, and of incompleteness; as if, with all the materials for world-making assembled, the creator had desisted, gone away and left everything on the point of being brought together, on the eve of being arranged into mountain, plain, plateau." Here, too, "the country was still waiting to be made into a landscape."

Such statements recall Jim Burden's initial reaction to the Nebraska prairie in *My Ántonia* (1918). As he rattles out to his grandparents' house at night, he peers over the side of the wagon. "There seemed to be nothing to see; no fences, no creeks or trees, no hills or fields. If there was a road, I could not make it out in a faint starlight. There was nothing but land: not a country at all, but the material out of which countries are made." Unformed, incomplete, lacking fences, trees, and hills, the land gives Jim Burden the feeling of being "over the edge" of the world, "outside man's jurisdiction."

From *PMLA* 84, no. 2 (March 1969). © 1969 by the Modern Language Association of America.

To this land Willa Cather brings the people who will struggle to make it give them first a subsistence, then a livelihood. In *O Pioneers!* the process is exemplified in the life of Alexandra Bergson, whose family had come to Nebraska when she was a child, whose faith and determination virtually force the land into yielding the riches which she so passionately believes it to possess. The early sections of *O Pioneers!* pose the question of survival sharply; the novel turns on the ultimately successful attempt of the pioneers to wrest a living from the land. In *My Ántonia,* Jim Burden's grandparents have achieved a degree of stability as the novel begins; it is the Shimerdas, the Bohemians, who move onto the prairie and make the early, elemental struggle that is the prerequisite of survival and success. With the efforts of her characters to subdue, to form, to complete the land, Willa Cather's novels of the prairie may properly be said to begin. Necessarily, then, Miss Cather writes about change, for if the people are not to be annihilated or forced into retreat by the land, the land must be altered by the efforts of the people.

The land, still menacing to the newcomer in its intransigence; the people of various backgrounds, whose object is to humanize, even domesticate, this land; the change, physical, economic, and social, consequent upon their efforts—such staple elements of Willa Cather's novels of the prairie go into the making of *My Ántonia.* But the novel has, of course, a special character of its own, an individuality that comes in large part from the Shimerdas; from their daughter Ántonia, who becomes a symbol of battered but undiminished human value; from Lena Lingard, soft, enticing, sensually eloquent; and, finally, from the narrator, Jim Burden, whose point of view defines the theme and structure even as it controls the tone of the novel.

From the time of the composition of *My Ántonia,* the role of Jim Burden has invited attention. Perhaps feeling the need to define that role more specifically, Willa Cather revised the preface of the novel for the reissue of 1926, making changes that altered Jim Burden's relation to the story he tells. In the 1918 preface, for example, Jim agrees to record his memories of Ántonia, which he has not thought of doing before; in the second preface, however, he is already at work on the manuscript before the meeting and conversation that supposedly take place with Willa Cather on the train. Such a change implies that something private and personal has been at work in the mind of Jim Burden, that the manuscript has taken initial shape because of an inner need to articulate the meaning of a valued, ultimately treasured, memory. Willa Cather has amended her first (prefatory) thoughts by bringing her narrator closer emotionally to the substance of the narrative.

Readers have continued to assess the role of Jim Burden because of its relevance to the structure of the novel as a whole. David Daiches, for example, believes that "the narrator's development goes on side by side with Ántonia's" and finds the symbolism uncertain at the conclusion: The final suggestion that this is the story of Jim and Ántonia and their relation is not really borne out by the story as it has developed. It begins as that, but later the strands separate until we have three main themes all going—the history of Ántonia, the history of Jim, and scenes of Nebraska life." The result, Daiches feels, and no mean achievement, is "a flawed novel full of life and interest and possessing a powerful emotional rhythm in spite of its imperfect structural pattern." E. K. Brown sees a potential problem in the choice of a man as narrator: Jim Burden "was to be fascinated by Ántonia as only a man could be, and yet he was to remain a detached observer, appreciative but inactive, rather than take a part in her life." The consequence of Willa Cather's effort to achieve these two not fully compatible effects is an emptiness "at the very center" of Jim's relation to Ántonia, "where the strongest emotion might have been expected to obtain." Stressing the function of the narrator, James E. Miller, Jr., believes that the "emotional structure of the novel may be discovered" in the drama of Jim Burden's "awakening consciousness," which shapes in the reader a sharpened awareness of cyclic fate that is the human destiny." John H. Randall III, in his impressive study of Willa Cather, would seem to agree with the implications of some of the previous arguments when he says that Jim Burden is more than "a first-person onlooker who is relating someone else's story." Randall develops the idea of a double protagonist, part Ántonia, who faces the future, part Jim Burden, who faces the past. Together, Jim and Ántonia make a complete, albeit "Janus-faced," personality.

If structural coherence is to be found in *My Ántonia,* the character of Jim Burden seems necessarily to be involved. As the story of Ántonia, the novel is quite rightly found inadequate; and even as the story of Ántonia and Jim Burden, the narrative strands, as Mr. Daiches indicates, tends to separate. For it is the story of Jim's Ántonia, and the meaning and implications of that term must somehow subsume the various elements of the novel. As I see it, the substance and quality of the narrative itself—at once evolving toward and conditioned by the image of Jim's Ántonia—provide a principle of unity that takes the special form of a drama of memory.

Jim Burden's drama of memory begins with his portrayal of the Shimerda family, who have arrived on the prairie from Bohemia at the same time Jim has come from Virginia to live with his grandparents after the death of his mother and father. The conditions of the agricultural frontier in Nebraska force the Shimerdas into a bleak, defensive existence.

They take up residence in a kind of cave, in front of which is a flimsy shed thatched with the wine-colored grass of the prairie. To Jim's grandmother the dwelling seems "no better than a badger hole; no proper dugout at all." But it is where the new family must live if they are to have shelter. On the fringe of civilization, overpowered by the utter strangeness of their environment, the Shimerdas face a contest for survival more in bewilderment than in desperation. For they have come unprepared. Mr. Shimerda, as Jim says, "knew nothing about farming"; a weaver by trade, he "had been a skilled workman on tapestries and upholstery materials" in his native land. We sense his confusion, his loss of identity, in his new surroundings. Awed by the magnitude of nature on the prairie, Jim Burden admits that "between that earth and that sky I felt erased, blotted out"; his statement evinces a deep feeling of insignificance, a sense of the radically diminished importance of the human being and his endeavors. This Jim can accept with the stoicism of youth: "I did not say my prayers that night," he writes; "here, I felt, what would be would be." Mr. Shimerda, however, can neither attain nor afford the luxury of resignation. For the prairie threatens him in subtle and profound ways. "Of all the bewildering things about a new country," writes Willa Cather in O Pioneers!, "the absence of human landmarks is one of the most depressing and disheartening." A citizen of the Old World, Mr. Shimerda cannot survive the loss of a society that was characterized by intellectual and artistic "landmarks." Faced with the necessity of making a new start from a point prior to any he had ever imagined, Mr. Shimerda has nothing with which to begin but his fiddle and an old gun given to him long ago for playing at a wedding. He dies from a lack of history, his suicide a testimony to the grim reality of the struggle imposed by frontier conditions.

In portraying the remaining Shimerda family, Willa Cather steadfastly avoids the trap of sentimentality. It would be a simple matter to resolve their problems with a rush of pity and a flood of tears, and the Burdens stand willing (almost determined) to help. But the Shimerdas (Mrs. Shimerda and Ambrosch particularly, but Ántonia also, to a degree) prove difficult to help. Embittered by their lot, they are shown to be unpleasant, ungrateful, and boastful; they brag of the old country and make comparisons invidious to the new. The sullen duplicity of Ambrosch leads finally to the harness incident, in which Ambrosch kicks at Jake Marpole and is felled by a blow from Jake's solid American fist. "They ain't the same, Jimmy," Jake says afterward, "these foreigners ain't the same. You can't trust 'em to be fair. It's dirty to kick a feller. You heard how the women turned on you—and after all we went through on account of 'em last winter! They ain't to be trusted. I don't want to see you get too thick with any of 'em." To which Jim responds with emotion: "I'll never be friends with them again, Jake."

Although such antipathy fades completely with time and understanding (the latter supplied principally by Mr. Burden), it typifies in a muted way some of the tensions implicit in American history. Earlier, on the train heading for Nebraska, Jake Marpole has approved Jim Burden's reluctance to go into the car ahead and talk with the little girl with "pretty brown eyes," as the conductor describes Ántonia; you are "likely to get diseases from foreigners," he tells Jim. Jake is a Virginian, an old American, showing his distrust of the newcomer. But a similar feeling could exist between immigrant groups. Otto Fuchs tells Jim's grandmother that "Bohemians has a natural distrust of Austrians." When she asks why, he replies: "Well, ma'am, it's politics. It would take me a long while to explain." Religion, too, could obviously provide a source of tension, though, again, the subdued tone of the narrative resolves such tensions quietly, and, in one case, with a final note of humor. When the Catholic Mr. Shimerda kneels and crosses himself before the Burdens' religiously decorated Christmas tree (decorated with candles and with a nativity scene sent to Otto Fuchs from Austria), Jim and his grandmother are apprehensive. Mr. Burden is staunchly Protestant, no friend to the pomps of popery: "He was rather narrow in religious matters," says Jim, "and sometimes spoke out and hurt people's feelings." The moment of crisis dissolves, however, when grandfather, as Jim says, "merely put his fingertips to his brow and bowed his venerable head, thus Protestantizing the atmosphere."

An unsentimental portrait of the Shimerdas thus is not only valid psychologically; it also allows us to glimpse the prejudices that were part of the human situation on the Nebraska prairie. Such feelings, however, are consistently set in a larger context of generosity; in March the Shimerdas occupy a new four-room house which their neighbors have helped them to build. They were now "fairly equipped," says Jim, "to begin their struggle with the soil." *Struggle* is, of course, the key word, for the Shimerdas' position can be made reasonably secure only by unremitting labor. Much of the necessary work, as we know, falls to Ántonia, whose fortunes in the Shimerda household are distinctly subordinate to those of Ambrosch, the oldest son. (It is for Ambrosch, Ántonia tells Jim Burden, that they have come to the United States.) Through Jim's eyes we see her as she grows coarse and muscular doing the work of a man on the farm. "She was too proud of her strength," he says, annoyed because Ántonia talks constantly to him about how much she can "lift and endure." Ambrosch gives her hard jobs and dirty ones as well, some of them "chores a girl ought not to do"; and Jim knows that "the farm-hands around the country joked in a nasty way about it." At the dinner table "Ántonia ate so noisily now, like a man, and she yawned often . . . and kept stretching her arms over her head, as if they ached." Jim's grandmother had said, "Heavy field work'll spoil that girl. She'll lose all her nice ways and get rough ones." To Jim, if not to his grandparents, "she had lost them already." Work has hardened his playmate of the previous autumn; virtually harnessed to the plow, developing a "draught-horse neck," she has little time for him. "I ain't got time to learn," she says when he informs her of the beginning of a new school term: "School is . . . for little boys." But the knowledge that her father would have been hurt by such an answer, and even more by the necessity for such an answer, brings tears to her eyes. Ántonia's determination to work for the immediate needs of her family molds her to the land. Fit material for a symbol, she is, I think we must in candor admit, already a bit too muscular for conventional romantic purposes.

The pace and emphases of the narrative in *My Ántonia* come of course from Jim Burden. As we know, the point of view is retrospective, and despite his disclaimer in the preface, Jim has both the perspective and the inclination to shape his material with care. Accordingly, book 1 has a definite pattern, that of the seasons: beginning with the autumn of his arrival, Jim takes us through the year to the fullness and heat of the following summer. Moreover, he portrays himself predominantly in terms of his reactions to the seasons during his first year on the prairie. The first section of the novel thus operates as a kind of rehearsal for nostalgia. For this year lives at the center of Jim's memory, never to be relived, never to be forgotten. It has for him an idyllic quality, a quality of tenderly remembered freedom and happiness resulting from his surrender to the forces of nature with which everyone else must contend. On the night of his arrival in Nebraska, we recall, Jim adopts an attitude of resignation: "here . . . what would be would be." The next day in his grandmother's garden he relaxes against a "warm yellow pumpkin," crumbles earth in his fingers, and watches and listens to nature. "Nothing happened," he says. "I did not expect anything to happen. I was something that lay under the sun and felt it, like the pumpkins, and I did not want to be anything more. I was entirely happy." He thinks of death (his parents, we remember, have recently died) and wonders if death makes us "a part of something entire." "At any rate," he concludes "that is happiness; to be dissolved into something complete and great."

Jim Burden, in short, makes an immediate surrender to nature in this garden with its ripe pumpkins. And his feeling of immersion in nature has a significant and permanent effect upon him, for he never loses his ability to appreciate the prairie in a personal way or his need to find happiness amid the ripeness and fulfillment of life. Though he must tell us of human hardship, Jim reveals his sense of rapture as he recalls and describes the seasons. "All the years that have passed," he says, "have not dimmed my memory of that first glorious autumn." The new country lay open before him, leading him to celebrate the splendor of the prairie in the last hour of the afternoon:

> All those fall afternoons were the same, but I never got used to them. As far as we could see, the miles of copper-red grass were drenched in sunlight that was stronger and fiercer than at any other time of the day. The blond cornfields were red gold, the haystacks turned rosy and threw long shadows. The whole prairie was like the bush that burned with fire and was not consumed. That hour always had the exultation of victory, of triumphant ending, like a hero's death—heroes who died young and gloriously. It was a sudden transfiguration, a lifting-up of day.

Jim's tone is reverential, replete with wonder, the product of a deep respect for the prairie and for the sunlight that brings it to ripeness.

Winter becomes primarily a time of taking refuge. Snow disguises the prairie with an insidious mask of white, leaving one, as Jim says later, with "a hunger for color." He is convinced that "man's strongest antagonist is the cold," though, in the security of his grandmother's basement kitchen, which "seemed heavenly safe and warm in those days," he can hardly experience its bitterness in the manner of the Shimerdas, who have only one overcoat among them and take turns wearing it for warmth. On cold nights, he recalls, the cry of coyotes "used to remind the boys of wonderful animal stories." A sense of adventure pervades Jim's life: by comparison, the life represented in books seems prosaic: the Swiss family Robinson, for example, "had no advantage over us in the way of an adventurous life"—and, later, Robinson Crusoe's life on the island "seemed dull compared with ours." If winter means taking refuge, it also satisfies the needs of Jim's young imagination and contributes the memory of adventure, a feeling of hardship happily domesticated by the company, the kitchen, and the stove "that fed us and warmed us and kept us cheerful."

Spring with the reawakening of the prairie and summer with its sense of fruition complete the cycle of the seasons. The pervasive lightness of spring delights Jim: "If I had been tossed down blindfold on that red prairie, I should have known that it was spring." And July brings the "breathless, brilliant heat which makes the prairies of Kansas and Nebraska the best corn country in the world. It seemed as if we could hear the corn growing in the night; under the stars one caught a faint crackling in the dewy, heavy-odored cornfields where the feathered stalk stood so juicy and green." These are to become the world's cornfields, Jim sees in retrospect; their yield will underlie "all the activities of men in peace or war."

A sense of happiness remembered pervades book 1, softening and mellowing the harsher outlines of the story Jim Burden has to tell. We are never really on the prairie with Jim, nor does he try to bring us there. Rather, he preserves his retrospective point of view and tells us what it was like for him on the prairie. "I used to love to drift along the pale-yellow cornfield," he says; and (as we have seen) "All the years that have passed have not dimmed my memory of that first glorious autumn"; and, again, though she is four years his senior and they have arrived on the prairie at the same time, Ántonia "had come to us a child, and now she was a tall, strong young girl." Such statements, and numerous devices of style throughout the novel, make a point of narrative distance and deliver the story to us in an envelope of memory. The style, that is to say, makes a deliberate—and almost total—sacrifice of immediacy in favor of the afterglow of remembrance. Even the scenes of violence are kept at a distance by having someone else tell them to Jim Burden; indeed, they are not so much scenes as inset stories, twice removed from the reader. Pavel's story of the wolves in Russia, Ántonia's story of the tramp who jumped into the threshing machine, the story of Wick Cutter's death (told by one of Ántonia's children)—all these contain a terror and a violence that is subdued by having them related to Jim as part of his story to us. In a similar indirect way we learn of Mr. Shimerda's death and of the seduction of Ántonia by Larry Donovan (whom we never meet). Only when Jim kills the snake, thus, in a sense, making the prairie safe for Ántonia, and when for Ántonia's sake he decoys himself in Wick Cutter's bedroom, are terror and violence (and in the latter case a mixture of comedy) brought close; and, in keeping with the retrospective point of view, these episodes, too, come to us through the spectrum of Jim's memory.

Defining the mode of Jim Burden's relation to his narrative leads us to see the special character of the novel itself and to judge it on its own terms rather than on any we might inadvertently bring to it. The statement of one critic that "something precious went into American fiction with the story of Ántonia Shimerda" is meant as a tribute to Willa Cather's novel; but it seems to me a misdirected tribute. For the novel does not present the *story* of Ántonia; it does, I believe, present a drama of memory by means of which Jim Burden tells us how he has come to see Ántonia as the epitome of all he has valued. At the time he writes, Jim Burden has made sense of his experience on the prairie, has seen the meaning it has and will have in his life. The early sections of *My Ántonia* present in retrospect the substance of meaning, conditioned throughout by Jim's assurance of that meaning. The latter sections justify his right to remember the prairie in the joyous manner of his youth. And the process of justification involves, most importantly, the image of Ántonia. This image acquires symbolic significance for Jim; embodying and justifying his memories, it validates nostalgia by giving his feeling for the past a meaning in the present.

By common consent, the "I" of the preface is taken to be Willa Cather. In the preface we learn that both to Jim Burden and Willa Cather, Ántonia, "more than any other person we remembered, . . . seemed to mean . . . the country, the conditions, the whole adventure of our childhood." Miss Cather says that she had lost sight of Ántonia, but that Jim "had found her again after long years." The preface thus establishes a relation between Jim Burden and Willa Cather outside the narrative that is important to the relationship of Jim and Ántonia within the narrative. Jim Burden becomes the imaginative instrument by means of which Willa Cather reacquaints herself with Ántonia: "He made me see her again, feel her presence, revived all my old affection for her." Her narrator, in short, serves Miss Cather as the vehicle for her own quest for meaning and value; his success measures her success; his symbol becomes her symbol; for his Ántonia is the Ántonia she has created for him.

If Jim Burden is to be made more than a heuristic phantom of the imagination, however, he must be given some kind of autonomy as a fictional character. Some drama, however quiet it may appear in retrospect, must play itself out in his life; some resolution must come inherently from the narrative. If we are to have a drama of memory, Jim's memory must somehow be challenged before it is vindicated in and by the image of Ántonia. The offstage challenges, those involved, for example, when Jim explains his twenty-year absence from the Nebraska prairie by saying "life intervened," afford little but material for conjecture and inference. The onstage challenge, however, affording material for analysis, enters Jim's room in Lincoln in book 3 in the very pretty form of Lena Lingard.

Lena Lingard first appears as one of the hired girls in book 2, along with Tiny Soderball, lesser characters such as the Bohemian Marys and the

Danish laundry girls, and, of course, Ántonia, who has come to Black Hawk to work for the Harlings. The move to Black Hawk does take Ántonia away from the prairie temporarily and tend to merge her importance with that of a group of girls. But by placing Ántonia and Lena Lingard together, as friends, Willa Cather can begin to suggest the different roles each of them will play in the life of Jim Burden. Moreover, Black Hawk provides a canvas on which Miss Cather can portray social consciousness and burgeoning social change in the Nebraska of this time. Despite the domestic vitality of the Harling family, readily available for Jim Burden (now living next door with his grandparents) to draw on, Black Hawk seems increasingly dull to Jim during his high school years. Small and very proper, the town makes life for young men an initiation into monotony. Except, of course, for the presence of the hired girls. These young women, all of foreign families, bring vivacity to Black Hawk; light-hearted, gay, and unpretentious, at the dances they are in great demand. More often than not, however, the proper young men must meet them surreptitiously, for the hired girls enjoy a lower social status than do the girls of the older American families in the town. Remarking on the social distinction, Jim Burden says that

> the daughters of Black Hawk merchants had a confident, unin-
> quiring belief that they were "refined," and that the country
> girls, who "worked out," were not. The American farmers in
> our county were quite as hard-pressed as their neighbors from
> other countries. All alike had come to Nebraska with little capi-
> tal and no knowledge of the soil they must subdue. All had
> borrowed money on their land. But no matter in what straits
> the Pennsylvanian or Virginian found himself, he would not let
> his daughters go out into service. Unless his girls could teach a
> country school, they sat home in poverty.

Kept from teaching by their inadequate knowledge of English, yet determined to help their families out of debt, the hired girls took domestic or similar employment. Some remained serious and discreet, says Jim, others did not. But all sent home money to help pay "for ploughs and reapers, brood-sows, or steers to fatten." Jim frankly admires such family solidarity, as a result of which the foreign families in the county were "the first to become prosperous." Today, he says, former hired girls are "managing big farms of their own; their children are better off than the children of the town women they used to serve." Pleased with their success, Jim feels paternal toward the entire group of girls and applauds the social change which accompanies their prosperity.

A single generation serves to bring about the kind of change Jim describes. In the Black Hawk of his youth, however, "the country girls were considered a menace to the social order." And surely none of them represented more of a menace than Lena Lingard. Demure, soft, and attractive, Lena radiates sexual charm without guile or effort. Before Jim has finished high school, both the married Ole Benson and the proper young bachelor Sylvestor Lovett have become driven, obsessed men because of her. Later, in Lincoln, her landlord, Colonel Raleigh, and the Polish violin teacher, Mr. Ordinski, are entranced by Lena and suspicious of Jim on her account. A blonde, Norwegian, Nebraskan Circe, Lena is a temptress who "gave her heart away when she felt like it," as Jim says, but "kept her head for business." If she does not literally turn her admirers into swine, she cannot prevent their appetites from giving them at times hardly less graceful postures. When dancing, says Jim, Lena moved "without exertion rather indolently." If her partner spoke to her, she would smile, but rarely answer. "The music seemed to put her into a soft, waking dream, and her violet-colored eyes looked sleepily and confidingly at one from under her long lashes. . . . To dance 'Home, Sweet Home' with Lena was like coming in with the tide. She danced every dance like a waltz, and it was always the same waltz—the waltz of coming home to something, of inevitable, fated return."

This is the Lena Lingard who walks into Jim's room in Lincoln, who dominates book 3 and seems very close to taking command of the novel. Like Ántonia, she has come from off the prairie; like Ántonia, too, she is generous and forthright. But unlike Ántonia, she makes a success of herself in business, as a fashion designer, first in Lincoln, later in San Francisco. And unlike Ántonia, she is determined not to marry, not to have a family. Lena's unconscious power to distract a man from whatever he may or should be doing exerts its influence on Jim during his final year at the University of Nebraska. He begins to drift, as he says, to neglect academic life, to live from day to day languidly in love with Lena. His mentor, Gaston Cleric, tells him to "quit school and go to work, or change your college and begin again in earnest. You won't recover yourself while you are playing about with this handsome Norwegian." To Gaston Cleric, Lena seems "perfectly irresponsible." In the light of her successful career, the judgment seems only partially valid, But Cleric is near the mark; Lena induces irresponsibility in the men who know her. And Jim is coming to know her well.

No overt antagonism exists between Lena and Ántonia, who are friends with a great deal in common. Yet Ántonia warns Jim in good-natured seriousness not to see too much of Lena; and when Ántonia discovers the manner in which Jim kisses Lena, she exclaims, "If she's up to any of her nonsense with you, I'll scratch her eyes out." Jim's dreams suggest the different roles the girls have in his life. At times he dreams of Ántonia and himself, "sliding down strawstacks as we used to do; climbing up the yellow mountains over and over, and slipping down the smooth sides into soft piles of chaff." He has also a recurrent dream of Lena coming toward him barefoot across a field, "in a short skirt, with a curved reaping-hook in her hand." "She was flushed like the dawn," he continues, "with a kind of luminous rosiness all about her. She sat down beside me, turned to me with a soft sigh and said, 'Now they are all gone, and I can kiss you as much as I like.'" Jim says, "I used to wish I could have this flattering dream about Ántonia, but I never did."

Jim's dream of Ántonia, we note, is based on the memory of shared childhood experiences, its sexual significance sublimated in terms of youthful fun and adventure. In Black Hawk, Ántonia has forbidden Jim to kiss her as he apparently kisses Lena, thereby rejecting his tentative gesture toward a relationship of adolescent sexuality. If he is to dream of Ántonia, he must put her in a context of their youth. His dream of Lena, however, more frankly sexual (with the reaping-hook suggestive of such things as fulfillment, castration, and the negation of time), has no context; it can take place only because "they are all gone." Jim's wish that he could have such a dream about Ántonia is part of his larger desire to have some definite, some formal relationship with her. As he says to her later, "I'd have liked to have you for a sweetheart, or a wife, or my mother or my sister— anything that a woman can be to a man." With Lena he drifts into a hedonistic relationship which carries with it the peril of irresponsibility. Somehow Lena always seemed fresh, new, like the dawn: "she wakened fresh with the world everyday," Jim says, and it was easy to "sit idle all through a Sunday morning and look at her." (Ántonia, of course, would be worshipping, not being worshipped, on a Sunday morning.) Like all enchantresses, Lena inspires a chronic forgetfulness. In an ultimate dramatic sense she would be fatal to memory. Consequently, she stands opposed to Ántonia, who will come to bear and to justify the burden of Jim's memory.

The structure of the narrative in book 3 suggests the charm that Lena exercises on Jim. Her entrance into his room, we recall, interrupts his study of Virgil. After she leaves, Jim thinks of all the country girls of Black Hawk and sees a relation between them and the poetry of Virgil: "If there were no girls like them in the world, there would be no poetry. I understood that clearly, for the first time. This revelation seemed to me inestimably precious. I clung to it as if it might suddenly vanish." The country girls are the raw material of poetry; and Jim feels that without them there can be no valid life of the mind. But when he sits down to his lesson for the following day, his newly acquired insight into the relation of "life" and "art" yields up his old dream of Lena, "like the memory of an actual experience." "It floated before me on the page like a picture," he recalls, "and underneath it stood the mournful line: '*Optima dies . . . prima fugit*'—the best days are the first to flee." Since this quotation from the *Georgics* serves as the epigraph of the novel, one has here, I believe, a sense of being close to the emotional center of Jim Burden's narrative. And yet Lena, not Ántonia, inspires the melancholy reflection. In the light of Jim's return to the prairie in book 4, and, especially, in book 5, one must conclude that, however tender, this is an unproductive nostalgia, an indulgence in romantic melancholy. Jim's dream of Lena only *seems* "like the memory of an actual experience." And the reality of memory rather than the artificiality of dream will finally serve him as a basis for happiness. Ultimately, the epigraph of the novel comes, as it must, to have fuller and deeper reference to the memory of Ántonia than to the dream of Lena.

Lena Lingard, it is important to see, retards the drama of memory. She represents in the novel not so much an anti-theme as a highly diversionary course of inaction. Promising repose, a blissful release from time, she can be identified by Jim with nothing but herself—which is to say that she does not, as does Ántonia, lend herself "to immemorial human attitudes which we recognize by instinct as universal and true."

Returning to Black Hawk after an absence of two years, Jim is "bitterly disappointed" that Ántonia, betrayed by Larry Donovan, has become "an object of pity," whereas Lena commands wide respect. Having gone to school [with] Lena, Jim has little immediate sympathy for one who cannot give her heart and keep her head for business. But he responds once again to the country, and its changes seem to him "beautiful and harmonious": "it was like watching the growth of a great man or a great idea." He goes to his old house on the prairie to hear about Ántonia from the Widow Steavans, sleeps in his old room, and confronts his only source of disappointment when he meets Ántonia working in the fields. While they talk, near Mr. Shimerda's grave, he perceives a "new kind of strength in the gravity of [her] face" and confesses that the idea of her is part of his mind. His old feeling for the earth returns, and he wishes he "could be a little boy again." Committed to his early definition of happiness, and thus to the idea of the prairie, and thus to that of Ántonia, he looks hard at her face, which, as he says, "I meant always to carry with me; the closest realest face, under all the shadows of women's faces, at the very bottom of my memory." The drama of memory has been resolved; Jim's memories will take form around the image of Ántonia.

Having placed so much value on a single memory, Jim feels both impelled and afraid to test its validity by a return to the prairie after an absence of many years. Throughout these years he has apparently maintained a kind of inner life; the image of Ántonia, suggesting youth and early happiness, has hardened into a reality which he fears to see shattered. But his visit to the Cuzaks in book 5 vindicates and fulfills the memory he has treasured. "Ántonia had always been one to leave images in the mind that did not fade—that grew stronger with time," he says; "in my mind there was a succession of such pictures." To indicate the value of the past to her, Ántonia produces for him her collection of photographs—of Jim, Jake Marpole, Otto Fuchs, the Harlings, even of Lena Lingard—as part of her family's heritage. Together they look through these photographs of old times, but in such a rich, lively context of the present, with children of all sizes laughing and crowding around to show that they, too, know of the early days, that past and present tend to merge in a dynamic new image of happiness that makes the future possible. Amid Ántonia's large family Jim feels like a boy again, but—and this I feel measures the final success of his return—he does not *wish* that he were a boy again, as he did in book 4. He has no more need to cling to the past, for the past has been transfigured like the autumn prairie of old. He has "not been mistaken" about Ántonia: "She was a rich mine of life, like the founders of early races." "She had only to stand in the orchard, to put her hand on a little crab tree and look up at the apples, to make you feel the goodness of planting and tending and harvesting at last." The somewhat contrived scene of Ántonia's children scrambling and tumbling up out of their new fruit cave, "a veritable explosion of life out of the dark cave into the sunlight" which makes Jim dizzy for a moment, proclaims the relationship between Ántonia and the prairie: both have yielded life in abundance; both have prevailed.

The unity of *My Ántonia* thus derives, I believe, from a drama of memory fulfilled in the present. Clearly the novel does not give us the story of Ántonia's life nor that of Jim's. Rather, it brings us to see the meaning of Ántonia to a man whose happiest days have been those of his youth, who, in the apotheosis of book 5, becomes reconciled to the present because of the enduring value of the past, even as he comes to possess that past anew because of the promise and vitality of the present. Jim's image of Ántonia has proved fruitful; his drama of memory is not only resolved but fulfilled. He has attained a sense of meaning in his narrative by confronting in retrospect the elements of his early world: from Jim we have learned of the land, the various people who work the land, and the change which the passing of a generation brings about; from Jim, too, we have had the portrait of the Shimerdas and that of Lena Lingard; and from Jim we have the triumphant image of Ántonia, "battered but not diminished," as his personal symbol of the value of human experience. The elements of the novel cohere in Jim Burden's drama of memory. And in Jim's Ántonia they are all subsumed.

Perspective as Structure and Theme in *My Ántonia*

David Stouck

In the "Introduction" to *My Ántonia,* the narrator, Jim Burden, says that his account of the Bohemian immigrant girl probably "hasn't any form." The apparent lack of coherent structure in the novel has bothered many critics, as well as its narrator, and a common conclusion has been that the book is seriously flawed as a result. René Rapin, an early critic of Willa Cather's work, singles out the disappearance of Ántonia in the central part of the book as a serious defect in the novel's structure. David Daiches finds that the book is flawed by the narrative point of view and also points to the disappearance of Ántonia "for long stretches at a time" as a major weakness in the book. Both Rapin and Daiches make this assessment because they view the central concern of the novel to be what Daiches calls "the development and self-discovery of the heroine." James Miller, Jr., however, argues that the novel is given form by the narrtor's sensibility, that the structure exists in the growth of Jim's awareness. I agree with Miller that in order to view the novel as having any consistent shape the reader must realize that its focus rests not simply on Ántonia, but rather on the narrator's perception of her (as suggested in the title). Miller, however, goes on to argue that the novel is given shape by three patterns of cyclical time operating throughout—the cycle of the seasons, the cycle of a human life, and the cycle of successive civilizations. This argument is interesting, although it leads him to overemphasize a fatalistic element in

From *Texas Studies in Literature and Language* 12, no. 2 (Summer 1970). © 1970 by the University of Texas Press.

the novel, which is surely subordinate to the narrator's sense of achievement at the novel's close.

Essentially the novel consists of scenes and episodes in the lives of Jim Burden and Ántonia, few of which are sustained beyond anecdotal length. The novel reaches beyond mere nostalgia largely because, in giving imaginative form to childhood experiences, Miss Cather attempts not only to capture the emotions invested in early memories, but also to reconcile these feelings with the inevitable sense of loss and disillusionment experienced by the adult. The technical problem she faced was that of organizing the memories of childhood so that what was timeless and valuable would emerge from them. This was solved in part by adopting the pastoral mode: the narrator returns to the prairie landscape of his childhood in search of a timeless, indestructible order where some permanent values might be found and guaranteed. Implicit in [a] pastoral, however, is the recognition that the fulfillment of one's longing for permanence depends paradoxically on the acknowledgment of mutability rather than an escape from it. This reconciliation of past and present—or, to put it another way, the establishment of permanent values in a world of transitory experience—is accomplished in the novel through a series of perspectives in time and place. The dramatic shape of the book is determined, not by cyclical patterns of time, but by the sequential and changing aspects of both time and place; these are the elements used to dramatize the narrator's dilemma, and they are ultimately the means of its resolution.

In a letter that touches on her method of composition in *The Professor's House,* Miss Cather gives us a suggestion of her purpose in this use of perspective. Here she explains that the effect she was trying to achieve with "Tom Outland's Story"—the middle section of *The Professor's House,* which is remote both in place and time from the main action of the rest of the book—is comparable to the effect achieved in the paintings of Dutch interiors, where a window looks out on the ships or the sea:

> Just before I began the book I had seen, in Paris, an exhibition of old and modern Dutch paintings. In many of them the scene presented was a livingroom warmly furnished, or a kitchen full of food and coppers. But in most of the interiors, whether drawing-room or kitchen, there was a square window, open, through which one saw the masts of ships, or a stretch of grey sea. The feeling of the sea that one got through those square windows was remarkable, and gave me a sense of the fleets of Dutch ships that ply quietly on all the waters of the globe—to Java, etc.

Although *My Ántonia* was written before the author made this observa-
tion, the device works the same way in the earlier novel. By placing the
subject in some kind of perspective a "sense" of its character and values
emerges more clearly. In *My Ántonia* the skillful ordering of temporal and
spatial elements is one of the important compositional devices upon which
the dialectic of the novel rests. Within the narrator's sensibility, changes in
place and time (marked by the five physical divisions of the book) evoke
the emotional response shared by narrator and reader and give the novel
its dramatic form.

II

The brief "Introduction" to *My Ántonia,* in which the "author" and
the narrator meet on a train in the Midwest and talk over their childhood
days in Nebraska, places the whole novel in the context of "things remembered." This introduction, where we learn about the narrator's present
life, puts a frame around the novel that throughout juxtaposes the present
with the past that is being recalled. Here we learn that Jim Burden is a
successful legal counsel for one of the great western railways and that,
though he spends much time traveling across the country, he has his permanent home in New York. We also learn that he is married but that his
wife is unsympathetic to his quiet tastes and the marriage is sterile and
meaningless for him. The brief character sketch of Jim's wife as a rich pa-
troness surrounded by a group of mediocre poets and painters prepares us
for that moment near the end of the novel when Ántonia, surrounded by
all her children, asks Jim how many he has. The introduction or frame,
then, places the narrator's memories in a perspective that creates dramatic
tension in the book. Later, as we read the narrator's account of his childhood and of his successful progress toward his legal ambitions, we are always aware at the same time of the futility of that success in the present.
The frame provides a perspective in place as well. Jim has left the Midwest
to pursue his career in the East, but, though he has a home in New York
City, it is not a real home to him and his traveling across country is a man-
ifestation of his spiritual and emotional unrest. This image is juxtaposed
dramatically with the happiness and security of Ántonia's farm in the
West. In the introduction, then, the "feelings" of loss and estrangement
(the controlling emotions in the book) are introduced through juxtaposi-
tions in time and place.

The body of the novel is divided into five sections (books), each of
which takes place at a different time and place in the narrator's life. Book
1 is the longest section (over one-third of the total novel) and describes the

first year that Jim spent on his grandparents' farm and his acquaintance with the Bohemian girl, Ántonia Shimerda. This is the crucial experience upon which the whole of the novel rests; books 2 to 5 are in essence a reexamination of that central experience from four different perspectives. The events and anecdotes that make up this first long section of the novel represent the narrator's earliest significant memories from childhood, and surrounding them is a sense of timelessness and spacelessness. This is not to suggest that Miss Cather has romanticized this section of the novel. The harshness of the landscape is always there and the summer yields to winter in a realistic seasonal progression. But the fact that this section takes the narrator through one complete cycle of the seasons (Jim arrives in Nebraska in early fall and the section ends late the following summer) places those experiences in the context of a cyclical rhythm that is ever recurring, and hence outside time in the sequential sense. When he first travels to his grandfather's farm in the wagon, a feeling of spacelessness characterizes his impression of the country:

> There seemed to be nothing to see; no fences, no creeks or trees, no hills or fields. If there was a road, I could not make it out in the faint starlight. There was nothing but land: not a country at all, but the material out of which countries are made. No, there was nothing but land—slightly undulating, I knew, because often our wheels ground against the brake as we went down into a hollow and lurched up again on the other side. I had the feeling that the world was left behind, that we had got over the edge of it, and were outside man's jurisdiction.

Jim remembers a similar feeling in his grandmother's garden:

> I wanted to walk straight on through the red grass and over the edge of the world, which could not be very far away. The light air about me told me that the world ended here: only the ground and sun and sky were left, and if one went a little farther there would be only sun and sky, and one would float off into them, like the tawny hawks which sailed over our heads making slow shadows on the grass.

Accompanying this sense of spacelessness is a tremendous sense of freedom that manifests itself in his observations of the landscape. He says that "the road ran about like a wild thing, avoiding the deep draws, crossing them where they were wide and shallow," and reflects that the "sunflower-bordered roads always seem to me the roads to freedom." After the killing of the snake, he says that "the great land had never looked to me so big and free." This sense of freedom, of life once lived beyond reach of a specific place and time, is focused in Jim's relation to Ántonia, whose wild, impulsive and generous nature is so much a part of the untamed landscape.

Time and place also function dramatically in book 1 in the stories told by the immigrants about their lives in the countries where they were born. There is the horrific little tale about the wolves and the wedding party told by the Russians, Pavel and Peter; there is the story of Ántonia's family when they still lived in Bohemia; and throughout there are references to times and places far away. But in this section of the novel these vistas in time and place do not function realistically to make the reader more aware of change and decay; rather they are charged with romantic suggestion of times and places full of wonder to a child. As the narrator recalls his night visit to the Russians' hut (when Pavel tells his story), his account of the setting with the red sunset, the bright stars, and the coyotes howling over the prairie gives the whole episode a romantic cast. The secretive nature of the story emphasizes this: "We did not tell Pavel's secret to anyone, but guarded it jealously—as if the wolves of the Ukraine had gathered that night long ago, and the wedding party been sacrificed, to give us a painful and peculiar pleasure." When Mrs. Shimerda gives the Burdens some dried mushrooms that she brought from Bohemia, the emotion this evokes in the narrator is again a romantic one: "I bit off a corner of one of the chips I held in my hand, and chewed it tentatively. I never forgot the strange taste; though it was many years before I knew that those little brown shavings, which the Shimerdas had brought so far and treasured so jealously, were dried mushrooms. They had been gathered, probably, in some deep Bohemian forest."

But in the following three sections of the novel the sense of freedom and romantic horizon disappears. The narrator becomes aware of time's passage and feels the restrictions of place. Though he is growing into manhood and moving out into the world, the world is becoming smaller and setting limitations on him. Book 2, "The Hired Girls," takes place three years later, when the Burdens have moved into the town of Black Hawk. In the first paragraph describing the town, the narrator refers to his "lost freedom" in leaving the farm. As time passes the narrator feels more and more repressed by the confines of the village and the frustrating mediocrity of its social life. In a despondent mood he reflects on the repression and lack of imagination in the small town:

On starlight nights I used to pace up and down those long, cold streets, scowling at the little, sleeping houses on either side, with their stormwindows and covered back porches. They were flimsy shelters, most of them poorly built of light wood, with spindle porch-posts horribly mutilated by the turning-lathe. Yet for all their frailness, how much jealousy and envy and unhappiness some of them managed to contain! The life that went on in them seemed to me made up of evasions and negations; shifts to save cooking, to save washing and cleaning, devices to propitiate the tongue of gossip. This guarded mode of existence was like living under a tyranny. People's speech, their voices, their very glances, became furtive and repressed. Every individual taste, every natural appetite, was bridled by caution. The people asleep in these houses, I thought, tried to live like the mice in their own kitchens; to make no noise, to leave no trace, to slip over the surface of things in the dark. The growing piles of ashes and cinders in the back yards were the only evidence that the wasteful, consuming process of life went on at all.

The narrator's feelings are again focused in Ántonia. In this section a number of the immigrant girls whom Jim had known in the country have come to town to work as domestics. To Jim these spontaneous, fun-loving girls are far superior to the repressed and imitative town girls who have been bred to social niceties and who seem utterly lacking in vitality. But the rough manners and irrepressible gaiety of Ántonia and her friends are frowned on by the strict decorum of the town, and they are treated very much as second-class citizens. The situation comes to a head when the Italian dancing pavilion is set up in Black Hawk. The town boys are attracted to the immigrant girls and choose them for partners at the Saturday night dances, but even Jim's grandmother, who is fond of Ántonia and the other girls, is upset when Jim goes dancing with them. The country girls are not socially acceptable in Black Hawk, and in order to "get on" they have to compromise. Ántonia leaves the Harlings' place because they disapprove of her dancing, and goes to work for Wick Cutter, who unsuccessfully tries to rape her. These unhappy and sometimes sordid incidents represent restrictions on the freedom that the narrator once shared with Ántonia in the country. In this section he also is faced with choosing what he will do in the future, and he begins sadly to realize that life will not always be as carefree and easy as the day when he picnics with Ántonia and her friends in the country. No one incident brings this section of the novel to a dramatic disclosure; the effect again is a cumulative one—"narrative without accent." The dramatic forces at work are simply those of place and time: the inevitable, increasing complexity of life for Jim as time passes, the limitations imposed by life in a small midwestern town.

In book 3, entitled "Lena Lingard," Jim has moved to Lincoln, where he is studying classics at the university. The central emotion of the novel—the increasing sense of loss and alienation as one grows older—is brought to the fore again in the narrator's relation to Antonia and the immigrant girls. Although Ántonia does not actually appear in this section, Lena Lingard, one of the country girls who has now moved to Lincoln to do dressmaking, visits Jim at his boarding house and revives in him all his feelings about his childhood with Ántonia. But even before Lena appears, as Jim reads and vast areas in time and space are opened up to him through scholarship, his mind continually wanders back to those days he spent as a child on the farm.

> Although I admired scholarship so much in Cleric, I was not deceived about myself; I knew that I should never be a scholar. I could never lose myself for long among impersonal things. Mental excitement was apt to send me with a rush back to my own naked land and the figures scattered upon it. While I was in the very act of yearning toward the new forms that Cleric brought up before me, my mind plunged away from me, and I suddenly found myself thinking of the places and people of my own infinitesimal past. They stood out strengthened and simplified now, like the image of the plough against the sun. They were all I had for an answer to the new appeal. I begrudged the room that Jake and Otto and Russian Peter took up in my memory, which I wanted to crowd with other things. But whenever my consciousness was quickened, all those early friends were quickened within it, and in some strange way they accompanied me through all my new experiences. They were so much alive in me that I scarcely stopped to wonder whether they were alive anywhere else, or how.

If the book has a dramatic turning point, I would suggest it lies here and in the following three paragraphs, where the epigraph, "the best days are the first to flee," is joined with Miss Cather's own purpose in the novel, expressed in the quotation from Virgil's *Georgics*: "I shall be the first—to bring the Muse into my country." Here the prevailing emotions of loss and estrangement are most effectively expressed, and here the underlying quest of both the author and the narrator is formulated—the search for some permanent form (for the author, it is the Muse) to embody and keep alive the values of one's personal past. The stage for this drama is in the narrator's mind; the dramatic principals are "the best days" (time) and "my country" (place). In spite of his love for the Nebraska countryside where he was raised, the narrator goes east to be with his tutor and eventually to enter law school there. Book 3 ends on the simple but significant note, "I joined Cleric in Boston. I was then nineteen years old."

When book 4, "The Pioneer Woman's Story," begins, two years have passed and the narrator has gone back to Black Hawk for the summer vacation. In this section the compromise and disillusionment of youth effected by the passing of time are outlined by the stories of the immigrant girls. Both Lena Lingard and Tiny Soderball have left Black Hawk to achieve material success in the world. Moving forward in time for a moment, Jim tells us that Tiny made a fortune in the Klondike and lives in San Francisco. She has never married or had a family. She had numerous exciting adventures in the Klondike, but "the thrill of them was quite gone. She said frankly that nothing interested her now but making money." And later Jim himself reflects that "she was like someone in whom the faculty of becoming interested is worn out." Lena has also done well financially and has gone to live near Tiny in San Francisco. Though she has not married either, she is considered a success by the people in Black Hawk because she has profited at dressmaking. In contrast to these girls who have embraced the repressive values of the town, Ántonia has followed the dictates of her emotions—the result of which is a child born out of wedlock. We have the feeling that all three girls have been betrayed in some way or other by their youthful dreams and by the passing of time. The importance of place emerges from the stories of Lena and Tiny; both girls have moved away from the country of their childhood, pursuing the illusion of success in farther fields. But life in the sophisticated world of San Francisco does not bring them any closer to happiness or fulfillment. Nor does running off to Denver to be married bring Ántonia the joy and security she hoped for. The myth of place—of leaving one's familiar surroundings to achieve success and happiness somewhere far away—is exploded by the contrasting picture of Ántonia on the farm at the end of the book.

III

In book 5, "Cuzak's Boys," the dramatic tension that has been created through the themes of transiency and alienation is resolved in the narrator's visit to Ántonia's farm. Twenty years have passed since Jim has seen

Ántonia, and in that time he has traveled great distances, at one point visiting Bohemia, where Ántonia was born. But he returns to the Nebraska country reluctantly, a disillusioned lawyer from the East, afraid of destroying one of the few meaningful realities remaining to him—the memory of his childhood:

> Perhaps it was cowardice that kept me away so long. My business took me West several times every year, and it was always in the back of my mind that I would stop in Nebraska some day and go to see Ántonia. But I kept putting it off until the next trip. I did not want to find her aged and broken; I really dreaded it. In the course of twenty crowded years one parts with many illusions. I did not wish to lose the early ones. Some memories are realities, and are better than anything that can ever happen to one again.

Jim fears losing the reality of his memories, but in fact his visit to Ántonia's farm bestows on them a permanent value that reaches beyond change in time and place. For Jim finds that though Ántonia has become aged and battered with the passing of the years, the real essence of her character has been preserved. In her life on the farm with her husband and children she has remained faithful to those instinctive values that she and Jim shared in their early years. Compared with Jim's sterile and cerebral existence, there is fruitfulness and harmony on Ántonia's farm. In what must certainly be the climax of the novel Jim connects his memories of Ántonia as a child with the picture of a woman whom he is now visiting, so many years later:

> In my memory there was a succession of such pictures, fixed there like the old woodcuts of one's first primer: Ántonia kicking her bare legs against the sides of my pony when we came home in triumph with our snake; Ántonia in her black shawl and fur cap, as she stood by her father's grave in the snowstorm; Ántonia coming in with her work-team along the evening sky-line. She lent herself to immemorial human attitudes which we recognize by instinct as universal and true. I had not been mistaken. She was a battered woman now, not a lovely girl; but she still had that something which fires the imagination, she could still stop one's breath for a moment by a look or gesture that somehow revealed the meaning in common things. She had only to stand in the orchard, to put her hand on a little crab tree and look up at the apples, to make you feel

> the goodness of planting and tending and harvesting at last. All
> the strong things of her heart came out in her body, that had
> been so tireless in serving generous emotions.

In this synthesis the "philosophic mind" of the narrator can at last view his personal memories as part of a greater and deeper life process. The values of those early years are rescued from the erosion of place and time because they derive from participation in those "immemorial human attitudes which we recognize by instinct as universal and true." They are embodied in Ántonia, whose life is spent in close communion with the timeless facts of existence—birth, growth and death—and in harmony with nature's changeless cycle of the seasons. The narrator has not escaped from the fact of his mortality, nor from the sadness produced by life's transience. In the field with Ántonia's children he feels again the haunting melancholy of place, "the loneliness of the farmboy at evening, when the chores seem everlastingly the same, and the world so far away." And when he waits for his train in Black Hawk, the passing of time still has its effect on him: "My day in Black Hawk was disappointing. Most of my old friends were dead or had moved away. Strange children, who meant nothing to me, were playing in the Harlings' big yard when I passed; the mountain ash had been cut down, and only a sprouting stump was left of the tall Lombardy poplar that used to guard the gate. I hurried on." But as he reflects later that day about his visit with Ántonia, he is consoled by the feeling that, for the first time, he has been able to recapture his childhood:

> This was the road over which Ántonia and I came on that night
> when we got off the train at Black Hawk and were bedded
> down in the straw, wondering children, being taken we knew
> not whither. I had only to close my eyes to hear the rumbling
> of the wagons in the dark, and to be again overcome by that
> obliterating strangeness. The feelings of that night were so near
> that I could reach out and touch them with my hand. I had the
> sense of coming home to myself, and of having found out what
> a little circle man's experience is.

The image of the circle, reconciling the two orders of time and space, symbolizes the final integration of the childhood and adult worlds. As a sophisticated, self-conscious man, the narrator cannot become a spontaneous Ántonia; but he does recognize the source of his dissatisfaction and the nature of those values which endure, and through this awareness he is reconciled to his sense of loss. The reconciliation is inherent in the novel's form, for the perception of value is effected by means of perspectives in time and place that illuminate what is transient and what endures. The final awareness is an emotional one, embodying both the loss and the achievement, and is sounded in the haunting last sentence of the book: "Whatever we had missed, we possessed together the precious, the incommunicable past."

The Forgotten Reaping-Hook: Sex in *My Ántonia*

Blanche H. Gelfant

Our persistent misreading of Willa Cather's *My Ántonia* rises from a belief that Jim Burden is a reliable narrator. Because we trust his unequivocal narrative manner, we see the novel as a splendid celebration of American frontier life. This is the view reiterated in [Terence Martin's] critique of *My Ántonia* and in [Randall's] comprehensive study of Cather's work: "*My Ántonia* shows fertility of both the soil and human beings. Thus, in a profound sense *My Ántonia* is the most affirmative book Willa Cather ever wrote. Perhaps that is why it was her favorite." Critics also elect it *their* favorite Cather novel: however, they regret its inconclusive structure, as did Cather when she declared it fragmented and unsatisfactory in form. David Daiches's complaint of twenty years ago prevails: that the work is "flawed" by "irrelevant" episodes and material of "uncertain" meaning. Both critical positions—that *My Ántonia* is a glorious celebration of American life and a defective work of art—must be reversed once we challenge Jim Burden's vision of the past. I believe we have reason to do so, particularly now, when we are making many reversals in our thinking. As soon as we question Jim's seemingly explicit statements, we see beyond them myriad confusions which can be resolved only by a totally new reading. This would impel us to reexamine Jim's testimony, to discover him a more disingenuous and self-deluded narrator than we supposed. Once we redefine his role, *My Ántonia* begins to resonate to new and rather shock-

From *American Literature* 43, no. 1 (March 1971). © 1971 by Duke University Press.

ing meanings which implicate us all. We may lose our chief affirmative novel, only to find one far more exciting—complex, subtle, aberrant.

Jim Burden belongs to a remarkable gallery of characters for whom Cather consistently invalidates sex. Her priests, pioneers, and artists invest all energy elsewhere. Her idealistic young men die prematurely; her bachelors, children, and old folk remain "neutral" observers. Since she wrote within a prohibitive genteel tradition, this reluctance to portray sexuality is hardly surprising. What should intrigue us is the strange involuted nature of her avoidance. She masks sexual ambivalence by certainty of manner, and displays sexual disturbance, even the macabre, with peculiar insouciance. Though the tenor of her writing is normality, normal sex stands barred from her fictional world. Her characters avoid sexual union with significant and sometimes bizarre ingenuity, or achieve it only in dreams. Alexandra Bergson, the heroine of *O Pioneers!,* finds in recurrent reveries the strong transporting arms of a lover; and Jim Burden in *My Ántonia* allows a half-nude woman to smother him with kisses only in unguarded moments of fantasy. Their dreams suggest the typical solipsism of Cather's heroes, who yield to a lover when they are most solitary, most inverted, encaptured by their own imaginations. As Alexandra dispels such reveries by a brisk cold shower, their inferential meaning becomes almost comically clear. Whenever sex enters the real world (as for Emil and Marie in *O Pioneers!*), it becomes destructive, leading almost axiomatically to death. No wonder, then, that Cather's heroes have a strong intuitive aversion to sex which they reveal furtively through enigmatic gestures. In *A Lost Lady,* when young Niel Herbert, who idealizes the Forrester's sexless marriage, discovers Mrs. Forrester's love affair, he vents his infantile jealousy and rage the only way he can—symbolically. While the lovers are on the phone, he takes his "big shears" and cuts the wires, ostensibly to prevent gossip, but also to sever a relationship he cannot abide. Ingenious in rationalizing their actions, Cather's heroes do not entirely conceal an underlying fear of physical love; and the connection between love and death, long undiscerned in Cather's work, can be seen as its inextricable motif. Even in her first novel, *Alexander's Bridge,* the hero's gratuitous death—generally thought to flaw the work—fulfills the inherent thematic demand to show physical passion as disastrous. Here, as in *O Pioneers!,* a later work, illicitness is merely a distracting irrelevance which helps conceal the fear of sexuality in all relationships. *O Pioneers!* reduces the interval between love and death until they almost coincide. At three o'clock, Emil races "like an arrow shot from the bow" to Marie; for the first time they make love; by evening, they are dead, murdered by the half-demented husband.

In *My Ántonia,* Jim Burden grows up with an intuitive fear of sex, never acknowledged, and in fact, denied: yet it is a determining force in his story. By deflecting attention from himself to Ántonia, of whom he can speak with utter assurance, he manages to conceal his muddied sexual attitudes. His narrative voice, reinforced by Cather's, emerges firm and certain; and it convinces. We tend to believe with Jim that his authoritative recitation of childhood memories validates the past and gives meaning to the present even though his mature years stream before him emptied of love, intimacy, and purpose. Memory transports him to richer and happier days spent with Ántonia, the young Bohemian girl who signifies *"the country, the conditions, the whole adventure of . . . childhood."* Because a changing landscape brilliantly illumines his childhood—with copper-red prairies transformed to rich wheatfields and corn—his personal story seems to epitomize this larger historical drama. Jim uses the coincidence of his lifespan with a historical era to imply that as the country changed and grew, so did he, and moreover, as his memoirs contained historical facts, so did they hold the truth about himself. Critics support Jim's bid for validity, pointing out that "*My Ántonia* exemplifies superbly [Frederick Jackson] Turner's concept of the recurring cultural evolution on the frontier."

Jim's account of both history and himself seems to me disingenuous, indeed, suspect; yet it is for this very reason highly pertinent to an understanding of our own uses of the past. In the introduction, Jim presents his memoirs as a spontaneous expression—unselected, unarranged, and uncontrolled by ulterior purpose: *"From time to time I've been writing down what I remember . . . about Ántonia. . . . I didn't take time to arrange it; I simply wrote down pretty much all that her name recalls to me. I suppose it hasn't any form, . . . any title, either."* Obviously, Jim's memory cannot be as autonomous or disinterested as he implies. His plastic powers reshape his experience, selecting and omitting in response to unconscious desires and the will. Ultimately, Jim forgets as much as he remembers, as his mind sifts through the years to retrieve what he most needs—a purified past in which he can find safety from sex and disorder. Of "a romantic disposition," Jim substitutes wish for reality in celebrating the past. His flight from sexuality parallels a flight from historical truth, and in this respect, he becomes an emblematic American figure, like Jay Gatsby and Clyde Griffiths. Jim romanticizes the American past as Gatsby romanticizes love, and Clyde money. Affirming the common, the prototypical American dream of fruition, all three, ironically, are devastated—Gatsby and Clyde die violently, while Jim succumbs to immobilizing regressive needs. Their relationship to the dream they could not survive must strike us oddly, for we have reversed their situation by surviving to see the dream shattered and the

Golden Age of American history impugned. Out of the past that Jim idealized comes our present stunning disorder, though Jim would deny such continuity, as Cather did. Her much-quoted statement that the world *broke* in 1922 reveals historical blindness mistaken for acuity. She denied that "the beautiful past" transmitted the crassness, disorder, and violence which "ruined" the present for her and drove her to hermitic withdrawal. She blamed villainous men, such as Ivy Peters in *A Lost Lady,* for the decline of a heroic age. Like her, Jim Burden warded off broad historical insight. His mythopoeic memory patterned the past into an affecting creation story, with Ántonia a central fertility figure, "a rich mine of life, like the founders of early races." Jim, however, stalks through his myth, a wasteland figure who finds in the present nothing to compensate him for the loss of the past, and in the outer world nothing to violate the inner sanctum of memory. "Some memories are realities, are better than anything that can ever happen to one again"—Jim's nostalgic conclusion rationalizes his inanition. He remains finally fixated on the past, returning to the vast and ineffaceable image that dominates his memoirs—the Nebraska prairie yielding to railroad and plough. Since this is an impersonal image of the growth of a nation, and yet it seems so personally crucial to Jim, we must be alerted to the special significance it holds for him. At the very beginning of the novel, we are told that Jim *"loves with a personal passion the great country through which his railway runs."* The symbolism of the railroad penetrating virgin fields is such an embarrassingly obvious example of emotional displacement, it seems extraordinary that it has been so long unnoted. Like Captain Forrester, the unsexed husband of *A Lost Lady,* Jim sublimates by traversing the country, laying it open by rail; and because he sees the land grow fertile and the people prosper, he believes his story to be a celebration.

But neither history's purely material achievement, nor Cather's aesthetic conquest of childhood material, can rightfully give Jim Burden personal cause to celebrate. Retrospection, a superbly creative act for Cather, becomes for Jim a negative gesture. His recapitulation of the past seems to me a final surrender to sexual fears. He was afraid of growing up, afraid of women, afraid of the nexus of love and death. He could love only that which time had made safe and irrefragable—his memories. They revolve not, as he says, about the image of Ántonia, but about himself as a child. When he finds love, it seems to him the safest kind—the narcissistic love of the man for himself as a boy. Such love is not unique to Jim Burden. It obsesses many Cather protagonists from early novels to late: from Bartley Alexander in *Alexander's Bride* to Godfrey St. Peter in *The Professor's*

House. Narcissism focuses Cather's vision of life. She valued above all the inviolability of the self. Romantically, she saw in the child the original and real self; and in her novels she created adult characters who sought a seemingly impossible reunion with this authentic being—who were willing to die if only they could reach somehow back to childhood. Regression becomes thus an equivocal moral victory in which the self defies change and establishes its immutability. But regression is also a sign of defeat. *My Ántonia,* superficially so simple and clear a novel, resonates to themes of ultimate importance—the theme of identity, of its relationship to time, and of its contest with death. All these are subsumed in the more immediate issue of physical love. Reinterpreted along these lines, *My Ántonia* emerges as a brilliantly tortuous novel, its statements working contrapuntally against its meanings, its apparently random vignettes falling together to form a pattern of sexual aversion into which each detail fits—even the reaping-hook of Jim's dream:

> One dream I dreamed a great many times, and it was always the same. I was in a harvest-field full of shocks, and I was lying against one of them. Lena Lingard came across the stubble barefoot, in a short skirt, with a curved reaping-hook in her hand, and she was flushed like the dawn, with a kind of luminous rosiness all about her. She sat down beside me, turned to me with a soft sigh and said, "Now they are all gone, and I can kiss you as much as I like."

In Jim's dream of Lena, desire and fear clearly contend with one another. With the dreamer's infallibility, Jim contains his ambivalence in a surreal image of Aurora and the Grim Reaper as one. This collaged figure of Lena advances against as ordinary but ominous landscape. Background and forefigure first contrast and then coalesce in meaning. Lena's voluptuous aspects—her luminous glow of sexual arousal, her flesh bared by a short skirt, her soft sighs and kisses—are displayed against shocks and stubbles, a barren field when the reaping-hook has done its work. This landscape of harvest and desolation is not unfamiliar; nor is the apparitional woman who moves across it, sighing and making soft moan; nor the supine young man whom she kisses and transports. It is the archetypal landscape of ballad, myth, and drama, setting for *la belle dame sans merci* who enchants and satisfies, but then lulls and destroys. She comes, as Lena does, when the male is alone and unguarded. "Now they are all gone," Lena whispers, meaning Ántonia, his threshold guardian. Keeping parental watch, Ántonia limits Jim's boundaries ("You know you ain't right to kiss me like that") and attempts to bar him from the dark unexplored country beyond boyhood with threats ("If I see you hanging around with Lena much, I'll go tell your grandmother"). Jim has the insight to reply, "You'll always treat me like a kid"; but his dream of past childhood games with Ántonia suggests that the prospect of perpetual play attracts him, offering release from anxiety. Already in search of safety, he looks to childhood, for adolescence confronts him with the possibility of danger in women. Characteristically, his statement that he will prove himself unafraid belies the drift of his unconscious feelings. His dream of Lena and the reaping-hook depicts his ambivalence toward the cycle of growth, maturation, and death. The wheat ripens to be cut; maturity invites death.

Though Jim has declared his dream "always the same," it changes significantly. When it recurs in Lincoln, where he goes as a university student, it has been censored and condensed, and transmuted from reverie to remembrance:

> As I sat down to my book at last, my old dream about Lena coming across the harvest-field in her short skirt seemed to me like the memory of an actual experience. It floated before me on the page like a picture, and underneath it stood the mournful line: *"Optima dies . . . prima fugit."*

Now his memory can deal with fantasy as with experience: convert it to an image, frame it, and restore it to him retouched and redeemed. Revised, the dream loses its frightening details. Memory retains the harvest field but represses the shocks and stubbles; keeps Lena in her short skirt, but replaces the sexual ambience of the vision. Originally inspired by the insinuative "hired girls," the dream recurs under the tranquilizing spell of Gaston Cleric, Jim's poetry teacher. As his name implies, Cleric's function is to guide Jim to renunciation of Lena, to offer instead the example of desire sublimated to art. Voluptuous excitement yields to a pensive mood, and poetry rather than passion engages Jim: "It came over me, as it had never done before, the relation between girls like those [Lena and "the hired girls"] and the poetry of Virgil. If there were no girls like them in the world, there would be no poetry." In his study, among his books, Lena's image floats before him on a page of the *Georgics,* transferred from a landscape of death to Virgil's bucolic countryside; and it arouses not sensual desire but a safer and more characteristic mood: nostalgia—"melancholy reflection" upon the past. The reaping-hook is forgotten. Lena changes from the rosy goddess of dawn to an apparition of evening, of the dimly lit study and the darkened theater, where she glows with "lamplight" rather than sexual luminosity.

This preliminary sublimation makes it possible for Jim to have an affair with Lena. It is brief and peculiar, somehow appropriating from the theaters they frequent an unreal quality, the aspect of play. In contrast to the tragic stage lovers who feel exquisitely, intone passionately, and love enduringly, they seem mere unengaged children, thrilled by make-believe people more than each other. "It all wrung my heart"; "there wasn't a nerve left in my body that hadn't been twisted"—Jim's histrionic (and rather feminine) outbursts pertain not to Lena but to *Marguerite Gauthier* as impersonated by "an infirm old actress." Camille's "dazzling loveliness," her gaiety and glitter—though illusory—impassion him far more than the real woman's sensuality. With Lena, he creates a mock-drama, casting himself in the stock role of callow lover pitted against Lena's older suitors. In this innocuous triangle, he "drifts" and "plays"—and play, like struggle, emerges as his memoirs' motif. Far from being random, his play is directed toward the avoidance of future responsibilities. He tests the role of lover in the security of a make-believe world where his mistress is gentle and undemanding, his adversaries ineffectual, and his guardian spirit, Cleric, supportive. Cleric wants him to stop "playing with this handsome Norwegian," and so he does, leaving Lena forever and without regret. Though the separation of the stage lovers Armand and Camille wracks them—"Lena wept unceasingly"—their own parting is vapid. Jim leaves to follow Cleric to Boston, there to study, and pursue a career. His period of enchantment has not proved one of permanent thrall and does not leave him, like Keats's knight, haggard and woebegone.

Nevertheless, the interim in Lincoln has serious consequences, for Jim's trial run into manhood remains abortive. He has not been able to bypass his circular "road of Destiny," that "predetermined" route which carries him back finally to Ántonia and childhood. With Lena, Jim seems divertible, at a crossroad. His alternatives are defined in two symbolic titles symbolically apposed: "Lena Lingard" and "Cuzak's Boys." Lena, the archetypal Woman, beckons him to full sexuality. Ántonia, the eternal Mother, lures him back through her children, Cuzak's boys, to perennial childhood.

If Jim cannot avoid his destiny, neither can he escape the "tyrannical" social code of his small town, Black Hawk, which permits its young men to play with "hired girls" but not to marry them. The pusillanimous "clerks and bookkeepers" of Black Hawk dance with the country girls, follow them forlornly, kiss them behind bushes—and run. "Respect for respectability" shunts them into loveless marriages with women of money or "refinement" who are sexless and safe. "Physically a race apart," the country girls are charged with sensuality, some of them considered "dangerous as high explosives." Through an empty conformist marriage, Jim avoids danger. He takes a woman who is independent and masculine, like Ántonia, who cannot threaten him as Lena does by her sheer femininity. Though Lena may be "the most beautiful, the most *innocently* sensuous of all the women in Willa Cather's works," Jim is locked into his fantasy of the reaping-hook.

Jim's glorification of Lena as the timeless muse of poetry and the unattainable heroine of romance requires a closer look. For while he seems to exalt her, typically, he works at cross-purposes to demean her—in his own involuted way. He sets her etherealized image afloat on pages of poetry that deal with the breeding of cattle (his memoirs quote only the last line here):

> So, while the herd rejoices in its youth
> Release the males and breed the cattle early,
> Supply one generation from another.
> For mortal kind, the best day passes first.
> (*Georgics,* book 3)

As usual, Jim remembers selectively—only the last phrase, the novel's epigraph—while he deletes what must have seemed devastating counsel: "Release the males." Moreover, the *Georgics* has only factitious relevance to Lena (though I might point out that it undoubtedly inspired Cather by suggesting the use of regional material and the seasonal patterning of book 1 of *My Ántonia*). If anything, the allusion is downright inappropriate, for Virgil's poem extols pastoral life, but Lena, tired of drudgery, wants to get away from the farm. Interested in fashion and sensuous pleasure, settling finally in San Francisco, she is not really the muse for Virgil.

Jim's allusion does have a subtle strategic value: by relegating Lena to the ideal but unreachable world of art, it assures their separation. Mismatched lovers because of social class, they remain irreconcilable as dream and reality. A real person, Jim must stop drifting and study; he can leave the woman while possessing Lena the dream in remembered reverie. Though motivated by fear and expediency (as much as Sylvester Lovett, Lena's fearful suitor in Black Hawk), he romanticizes his actions, eluding the possibility of painful self-confrontation. He veils his escape by identifying secretly with the hero Armand Duval, also a mismatched lover, blameless, whose fervid affair was doomed from the first. But as a lover, Jim belongs as much to comedy as to melodrama. His affair fits perfectly within the conventions of the comedy of manners: the sitting room, Lena's "stiff little parlour"; the serving of tea; the idle talk of clothes and fashion;

the nuisance pet dog Prince; the minor crises when the fatuous elder lovers intrude—the triviality. Engaged with Lena in this playacting, Jim has much at stake—nothing less than his sexuality. Through the more serious drama of a first affair, he creates his existential self: an adult male who fears a sexual woman. Through his trivial small-town comedy of manners, he keeps from introspection. He is drifting but busy, too much preoccupied with dinner parties and theater dates to catch the meaning of his drift. His mock romance recalls the words he had used years earlier to describe a childhood "mock adventure": "the game was fixed." The odds are against his growing up, and the two mock episodes fall together as *pseudo-initiations* which fail to make him a man.

Jim's mock adventure occurs years back as he and Ántonia explore a series of interconnected burrows in prairie-dog-town. Crouched with his back to Ántonia, he hears her unintelligible screams in a foreign tongue. He whirls to discover a huge rattler coiling and erecting to spring. "Of disgusting vitality," the snake induces fear and nausea: "His abominable muscularity, his loathsome, fluid motion, somehow made me sick." Jim strikes violently and with revulsion, recognizing even then an irrational hatred stronger than the impulse for protection. The episode—typically ignored or misunderstood—combines elements of myth and dream. As a dragon slaying, it conforms to the monomyth of initiation. It has a characteristic "call to adventure" (Ántonia's impulsive suggestion); a magic weapon (Peter's spade); a descent into a land of unearthly creatures (prairie-dog-town); the perilous battle (killing the snake); the protective tutelary spirit (Ántonia); and the passage through the rites to manhood ("You now a big mans"). As a test of courage, Jim's ordeal seems authentic, and critical opinion declares it so: "Jim Burden discovers his own hidden courage and becomes a man in the snake-killing incident." But even Jim realizes that his initiation, like his romance later, is specious, and his accolade unearned: "it was a mock adventure; the game . . . fixed . . . by chance, as . . . for many a dragon-slayer."

As Jim accepts Ántonia's praise, his tone becomes wry and ironic, communicating a unique awareness of the duplicity in which he is involved. Ántonia's effect upon Jim seems to me here invidious because her admiration of his manhood helps undermine it. Pronouncing him a man, she keeps him a boy. False to her role as tutelary spirit, she betrays him from first to last. She leads him into danger, fails to warn him properly, and finally, by validating the contest, closes off the road to authentic initiation and maturity.

Jim's exploration "below the surface" of prairie-dog-town strikes me as a significant mimetic act, a burrowing into his unconscious. Who is he "below the surface"? In which direction do his buried impulses lead? He acts out his quest for self-knowledge symbolically: if he could dig deep enough he would find a way through this labyrinth and learn the course of its hidden channels—whether "they ran straight down, or were horizontal . . . whether they had underground connections." Projecting upon the physical scene his adolescent concern with self, he speaks an analytic and rational language—but the experience turns into nightmare. Archetypal symbol of "the ancient, eldest Evil," the snake forces him to confront deeply repressed images, to acknowledge for the only time the effect of "horrible unconscious memories."

The sexual connotations of the snake incident are implicit. Later in Black Hawk they become overt through another misadventure—Wick Cutter's attempted rape of Jim, whom he mistakes for Ántonia. This time the sexual attack is literal. Wick Cutter, an old lecher, returns in the middle of the night to assault Ántonia, but meanwhile, persuaded by Ántonia's suspicions, Jim has taken her place in bed. He becomes an innocent victim of Cutter's lust and fury at deception. Threatened by unleashed male sex—the ultimate threat—he fights with primordial violence, though again sickened with disgust. Vile as the Cutter incident is—and it is also highly farcical—Jim's nausea seems an overreaction, intensified by his shrill rhetoric and unmodulated tone. Unlike the snake episode, this encounter offers no rewards. It simply reduces him to "a battered object," his body pommeled, his face swollen. His only recognition will be the laughter of the lubricious "old men at the drugstore." Again Ántonia has lured him into danger and exposed him to assault. Again he is furious: "I felt that I never wanted to see her again. I hated her almost as much as I hated Cutter. She had let me in for all this disgustingness." Through Wick Cutter, the sexual urge seems depraved, and more damning, ludicrous. No male in the novel rescues sex from indignity or gives it even the interest of sheer malevolence (as, for example, Ivy Peters does in *A Lost Lady*).

Also unexempt from the dangers of sex, Ántonia is seduced, exploited, and left with an illegitimate child. When finally she marries, she takes not a lover but a friend. To his relief, Jim finds husband and wife "on terms of easy friendliness, touched with humour." Marriage as an extension of friendship is Cather's recurrent formula, defined clearly, if idiosyncratically, by Alexandra in *O Pioneers!*: "I think when friends marry, they are safe." Turning words to action, Alexandra marries her childhood friend, as does Cecile in *Shadows on the Rock*—an older man whose passion has been expended on another woman. At best, marriage has dubious value in Cather's fiction. It succeeds when it seems least like marriage, when it remains sexless, or when sex is only instrumental to procreation. Jim accepts Ántonia's marriage for its "special mission" to bring forth children.

Why doesn't he take on this mission? He celebrates the myth of creation but fails to participate. The question has been raised bluntly by critics (though left unanswered): "Why had not Jim and Ántonia loved and married?" When Ántonia, abandoned by Donovan, needs Jim most, he passionately avers, "You really are a part of me": "I'd have liked to have you for a sweetheart, or a wife, or my mother or my sister—anything that a woman can be to a man." Thereupon he leaves—not to return for twenty years. His failure to seize the palpable moment seems to one critic responsible for the emotional vacuum of Jim's life: "At the very center of his relation with Ántonia there is an emptiness where the strongest emotion might have been expected to gather." But love for a woman is not Jim's "strongest emotion," cannot mitigate fear, nostalgia, or even simple snobbery. Nothing in Jim's past prepares him for love or marriage, and he remains in effect a pseudobachelor (just as he is a pseudolover), free to design a future with Ántonia's family that excludes his wife. In his childhood, his models for manhood are simple regressive characters, all bachelors, or patently unhappy married men struggling, like Mr. Shimerda, Chris Lingard, and Ole the Swede, for and against their families. Later in Black Hawk, the family men seem merely vapid, and prophetically suburban, pushing baby-carriages, sprinkling lawns, paying bills, and driving about on Sundays. Mr. Harling, Ántonia's employer in Black Hawk, seems different; yet he only further confuses Jim's already confused sense of sexual roles, for he indulges his son while he treats his daughter as a man, his business partner. With Ántonia, his "hired girl," Mr. Harling is repressive, a kind of superego, objecting to her adolescent contacts with men—the dances at Vannis's tent, the evening walks, the kisses and scuffles on the back porch. "I want to have my fling, like the other girls," Ántonia argues, but Harling insists she quit the dances or his house. Ántonia leaves, goes to the notorious Cutter, and then to the seductive arms of Larry Donovan—with consequences that are highly instructive to Jim, that can only reinforce his inchoate fears. Either repression of sex or disaster: Jim sees these alternatives polarized in Black Hawk, and between them he cannot resolve his ambivalence. Though he would like Ántonia to become a woman, he wants her also to remain asexual.

By switching her sexual roles, Ántonia only adds to his confusion. As "hired girl" in Black Hawk and later as Cuzak's wife, she cooks, bakes, sews, and rears children. Intermittently, she shows off her strength and endurance in the fields, competing with men. Even her name changes gender—no adventitious matter, I believe; it has its masculine variant, Tony, as Willa Cather had hers, Willie. Cather's prototype for Ántonia, Annie Pavelka, was a simple Bohemian girl; though their experiences are similar, Ántonia Shimerda is Cather's creation—an ultimately strange bisexual. She shares Cather's pride in masculinity and projects both her and Jim's ambivalent sexual attitudes. Cather recalled that "much of what I knew about Annie came from the talks I had with young men. She had a fascination for them." In the novel, however, Lena fascinates men while Ántonia toils alongside them. "I can work like mans now," she announces when she is only fifteen. In the fields, says Jim, "she kept her sleeves rolled up all day, and her arms and throat were burned as brown as a sailor's. Her neck came up strongly out of her shoulders, like the bole of a tree out of the turf. One sees that draught-horse neck among the peasant women in all old countries." Sailor, tree, draught-horse, peasant—hardly seductive comparisons, hardly conducive to fascination. Ántonia's illegitimate pregnancy brutalizes her even more than heavy farmwork. Her punishment for sexual involvement—and for the breezy pleasures of courtship—is thoroughgoing masculinization. Wearing "a man's long overcoat and boots, and a man's felt hat," she does "the work of a man on the farm," plows, herds cattle. Years later, as Cuzak's wife, her "inner glow" must compensate for the loss of her youthful beauty, the loss, even, of her teeth. Jim describes her finally as "a stalwart, brown woman, flat-chested, her curly brown hair a little grizzled"—his every word denuding her of sensual appeal.

This is not to deny that at one time Jim found Ántonia physically desirable. He hints that in Black Hawk he had kissed her in a more than friendly way—and had been rebuffed. But he is hardly heartbroken at their impasse, for his real and enduring love for her is based not on desire but on nostalgia. Childhood memories bind him more profoundly than passion, especially memories of Mr. Shimerda. In their picnic reunion before Jim departs for Lincoln, Ántonia recounts her father's story of transgression, exile, and death. Her miniature tale devolves upon the essential theme of destructive sex. As a young man, her father succumbs to desire for the family's servant girl, makes her pregnant, marries her against his parents' wishes, and becomes thereby an outcast. His death on the distant prairie traces back to an initial sexual act which triggers inexorable consequences. It strips him of all he values: his happy irresponsible bachelor life with the trombone-player he "loves"; his family home in beautiful Bohemia; his vocation as violinist when he takes to homesteading in Nebraska; and his joy in life itself. For a while, a few desultory pleasures could rouse him from apathy and despair. But in the end, he finds the pattern of his adult life, as many Cather characters do, unbearable, and he longs for escape. Though Ántonia implies that her poppa's mistake was to marry, especially outside his social class (as Jim is too prudent to do), the marriage comes about through his initial sexual involvement. Once Mr. Shimerda acts upon sexual impulse, he is committed to a woman who alienates him from himself; and it is loss of self, rather than the surmountable hardships of pioneer life, which induces his despair. Suicide is his final capitulation to destructive forces he could have escaped only by first abnegating sex.

Though this interpretation may sound extreme—that the real danger to man is woman, that his protection lies in avoiding or eliminating her—it seems to me the essence of the most macabre and otherwise unaccountable episode in *My Ántonia*. I refer to that grisly acting out of male aversion, the flashback of Russian Pavel feeding the bride to the wolves. I cannot imagine a more graphic representation of underlying sentiments than we find here. Like most of the episodes in Jim's memoirs, this begins innocently, with the young bride drawing Peter, Pavel, and other guests to a nearby village for her wedding. But the happy evening culminates in horror; for the wolves are bad that year, starving, and when the guests head for home they find themselves rapidly pursued through a landscape of terror. Events take on the surreality of nightmare as black droves run like streaks of shadows after the panicking horses, as sledges overturn in the snow, and mauled and dying wedding guests shriek. Fast as Pavel drives his team, it cannot outrun the relentless "back ground-shadows," images of death. Pavel's murderous strategy to save himself and Peter is almost too inhuman to imagine: to allay the wolves and lighten his load, he wrests the bride from the struggling groom, and throws her, living bait, to the wolves. Only then does his sledge arrive in safety at his village. The tale holds the paradigm for Mr. Shimerda's fate—driven from home because of a woman, struggling for survival against a brutal winter landscape, pursued by regret and despair to death. The great narrative distance at which this episode is kept from Jim seems to me to signify its explosiveness, the need to handle with care. It is told to Jim by Ántonia, who overhears Peter telling it to Mr. Shimerda. Though the vignette emerges from this distance—and through Jim's obscuring nostalgia—its gruesome meaning focuses the apparently disjunct parts of the novel, and I find it inconceivable that critics consider it "irrelevant." The art of *My Ántonia* lies in the subtle and inevitable relevance of its details, even the most trivial, like the picture Jim chooses to decorate a Christmas book for Ántonia's little sister: "I took 'Napoleon Announcing the Divorce to Josephine' for my frontispiece." In one way or another, the woman must *go*.

To say that Jim Burden expresses castration fears would provide a facile conclusion: and indeed his memoirs multiply images of sharp instruments and painful cutting. The curved reaping-hook in Lena Lingard's hands centralizes an overall pattern that includes Peter's clasp-knife with which he cuts all his melons; Crazy Mary's corn-knife (she "made us feel how sharp her blade was, showing us very graphically just what she meant to do to Lena"); the suicidal tramp "cut to pieces" in the threshing machine; and wicked Wick *Cut*ter's sexual assault. When Lena, the essence of sex, appears suddenly in Black Hawk, she seems to precipitate a series of violent recollections. First Jim remembers Crazy Mary's pursuit of Lena with her sharpened corn-knife. Then Ántonia recalls the story of the crazy tramp in details which seem to me unconsciously reverberating Jim's dream. Like Jim, Ántonia is relaxed and leaning against a strawstack; similarly, she sees a figure approach "across the stubble"—significantly, his first words portend death. Offering to "cut bands," within minutes he throws himself into the threshing machine and is "cut to pieces." In his pockets the threshers find only "an old penknife" and the "wish-bone of a chicken." Jim follows this anecdote with a vignette of Blind d'Arnault, a black musician who, as we shall see, represents emasculation; Jim tells how children used to tease the little blind boy and try "to get his chicken-bone away." Such details, I think, should not be considered fortuitous or irrelevant; and critics who have persisted in overlooking them should note that they are stubbornly there, and in patterned sequence.

I do not wish to make a case history of Jim Burden or a psychological document of *My Ántonia,* but to uncover an elusive underlying theme— one that informs the fragmentary parts of the novel and illuminates the obsession controlling Cather's art. For like most novelists, Cather writes out of an obsessive concern to which her art gives various and varied expression. In *My Ántonia,* her consummate work, that obsession has its most private as well as its most widely shared meanings. At the same time that the novel is highly autobiographical, it is representatively American in its material, mood, and unconscious uses of the past. In it, as in other novels, we can discover that Cather's obsession had to do with the assertion of self. This is the preoccupation of her protagonists who in their various ways seek to assert their identity, in defiance, if necessary, of others, of convention, of nature, of life itself. Biographers imply that Cather's life represented a consistent pursuit of autonomy, essential, she believed, to her survival as an artist. Undoubtedly, she was right; had she given herself to marriage and children, assuming she could, she might have sacrificed her chance to write. Clearly, she identified writing with masculinity, though which of the two constituted her fundamental drive is a matter of psychological dynamics we can never really decide. Like Ántonia, she displayed strong masculine traits, though she loved also feminine frilleries and the art of cuisine. All accounts of her refer to her "masculine personality"—her mannish dress, her deep voice, her energetic stride; and even as a child she affected boyish clothes and cropped hair. Too numerous to document, such references are a running motif throughout the accounts of Mildred Bennett, Elizabeth Sergeant, and E. K. Brown. Their significance is complex and perhaps inescapable, but whatever else they mean, they surely demonstrate Cather's self-assertion: she would create her own role in life, and if being a woman meant sacrificing her art, then she would lead a private and inviolate life in defiance of convention.

Her image of inviolability was the *child*. She sought quaintly, perhaps foolishly, to refract this image through her person when she wore a schoolgirl costume. The Steichen photograph of her in middy blouse is a familiar frontispiece to volumes of her work; and she has been described as characteristically "at the typewriter, dressed in a childlike costume, a middy blouse with navy bands and tie and a duck skirt." In life, she tried to hold on to childhood through dress; in art, through a recurrent cycle of childhood, maturity, and childhood again: the return effected usually through memory. Sometimes the regressive pattern signalized a longing for death, as in *The Professor's House* and *Death Comes for the Archbishop;* always it revealed a quest for reunion with an original authentic self. In *My Ántonia*, the prologue introduces Ántonia and the motif of childhood simultaneously, for her name is linked with *"the country, the conditions, the whole adventure of . . . childhood."* The memoirs proper open with the children's journey into pristine country where men are childlike or project into life characters of the child's imagination: like Jake who "might have stepped out of the pages of 'Jesse James.' " The years of maturity comprise merely an interim period—and in fact, are hardly dealt with. For Jim, as for Cather, the real meaning of time is cyclical, its purpose to effect a return to the beginning. Once Jim finds again "the first road" he traveled as a wondering child, his story ends. Hardly discernible, this road returns him to Ántonia, and through her, to his real goal, the enduring though elusive image of his original self which Cather represents by his childhood shadow. Walking to Ántonia's house with her boys—feeling himself almost a boy again—Jim merges with his shadow, the visible elongation of self.

At last, his narcissistic dream comes to fulfillment: "It seemed, after all, so natural to be walking along a barbed-wire fence beside the sunset, toward a red pond, and to see my shadow moving along at my right, over the close-cropped grass." Just as the magnified shadow of plow against sky— a blazing key image—projects his romantic notion of the West, so "two long shadows [that] flitted before or followed after" symbolize his ideal of perennial children running through, imaged against, and made one with the prairie grass.

Jim's return "home" has him planning a future with Cuzak's boys that will recapitulate the past: once more he will sleep in haylofts, hunt "up the Niobrara," and travel the "Bad Lands." Play reenters as his serious concern, not the sexual play of imminent manhood, but regressive child's play. In a remarkable statement, Jim says: "There were enough Cuzaks to play with for a long while yet. Even after the boys grew up, there would always be Cuzak himself!" A [1969] article on *My Ántonia* misreads this conclusion: "[though] Jim feels like a boy again . . . he does not *wish* that he were a boy again. . . . He has no more need to cling to the past, for the past has been transfigured like the autumn prairie of old." Such reasoning falls in naively with Jim's self-deception, that the transformation of the land to country somehow validates his personal life. Jim's need to reenter childhood never relents, becomes even more urgent as he feels adult life vacuous. The years have not enriched him, except with a wealth of memories—"images in the mind that did not fade—that grew stronger with time." Most precious in his treasury of remembered images is that of a boy of ten crossing the prairie under "the complete dome of heaven" and finding sublimity in the union of self with earth and sky. An unforgettable consummation, never matched by physical union, he seeks to recreate it through memory. Jim's ineffable desire for a child more alive to him than his immediate being vibrates to a pathetic sense of loss. I believe that we may find this irretrievable boy in a photograph of young *Willie Cather,* another child who took life from imagination and desire.

In a later novel, *The Professor's House,* Cather rationalizes her cathexis on childhood through the protagonist's musings, at which we might glance briefly. Toward the end of his life, Professor Godfrey St. Peter discovers he has two identities: that of his "original" self, the child; and of his "secondary" self, the man in love. To fulfill himself, "the lover" creates a meretricious "design" of marriage, children, and career, now, after thirty years, suddenly meaningless. The Professor's cyclic return to his real and original self begins with solitary retrospection. All he wants is to "be alone"—to repossess himself. For, having yielded through love to another, he has lost "the person he was in the beginning." Now before he dies, he longs for his original image as a child, an image that returns to him in moments of "vivid consciousness" or of remembrance. Looking back, the Professor sees the only escape from a false secondary life to be through premature death: death of the sexual man before he realizes his sexuality and becomes involved in the relationships it demands. This is the happy fate of his student Tom Outland, who dies young, remaining inviolate, pure, and most important, self-possessed: "He seemed to know . . . he was solitary and must always be so; he had never married, never been a father. He was earth, and would return to earth."

This Romantic mystique of childhood illuminates the fear of sex in Cather's world. Sex unites one with another. Its ultimate threat is loss of self. In Cather's construct, naively and of course falsely, the child is asexual, his love inverted, his identity thus intact. Only Ántonia manages to grow older and retain her original integrity. Like Tom Outland, her affinity is for the earth. She "belongs" to the farm, is one with the trees, the flowers, the rye and wheat she plants. Though she marries, Cuzak is only "the instrument of Ántonia's special mission." Through him she finds a self-fulfillment that excludes him. Through her, Jim hopes to be restored to himself.

The supreme value Jim and other Cather characters attribute to "old friendships" reflects a concern with self. Old friends know the child immanent in the man. Only they can have communion without causing self-estrangement, can marry "safely." They share "the precious, the incommunicable past"—as Jim says in his famous final words. But to keep the past so precious, they must romanticize it; and to validate childhood, they must let memory filter its experiences through the screen of nostalgia. Critics have wondered whether Jim Burden is finally the most suitable narrator for *My Ántonia*. I submit that Cather's choice is utterly strategic. For Jim, better than any other character, could control his memories, since only he knows of but does not experience the suffering and violence inherent in his story. And ultimately, he is not dealing with a story as such, but with residual "images in the mind." *My Ántonia* is a magnificent and warped testimony to the mind's image-making power, an implicit commentary on how that creative power serves the mind's need to ignore and deny whatever is reprehensible in whatever one loves. Cather's friend and biographer [Elizabeth Sergeant] said of her, "There was so much she did not want to see and saw not." We must say the same of Jim Burden, who held painful and violent aspects of early American life at safe distance, where finally he could not see them.

Jim's vignette of Blind d'Arnault, the black piano player who entertains at Black Hawk, is paradigmatic of his way of viewing the past. Its factual scaffolding (whether Cather's prototype was Blind Boone, Blind Tom, or a "composite of Negro musicians") seems to me less important than its tone. I find the vignette a work of unconscious irony as Jim paints d'Arnault's portrait but meanwhile delineates himself. The motif of blindness compounds the irony. D'Arnault's is physical, as though it is merely futile for him to see a world he cannot enter. Jim's is moral: an unawareness of his stereotyped, condescending, and ultimately invidious vision. Here, in his description of the black man, son of a slave, Jim's emblematic significance emerges as shamefully he speaks for himself, for Cather, and for most of us:

> [His voice] was the soft, amiable Negro voice, like those I remembered from early childhood, with the note of docile subservience in it. He had the Negro head, too; almost no head at all, nothing behind the ears but the folds of neck under close-cropped wool. He would have been repulsive if his face had not been so kindly and happy. It was the happiest face I had seen since I left Virginia.

Soft, amiable, docile, subservient, kindly, happy—Jim's image, as usual, projects his wish-fulfillment; his diction suggests an unconscious assuagement of anxiety, also. His phrase of astounding insult and innocence—"almost no head at all"—assures him that the black man should not frighten, being an incomplete creature, possessed, as we would like to believe, of instinct and rhythm, but deprived of intellect. Jim's final hyperbole registers his fear of this alien black face saved from repulsiveness only by a toothy servile smile (it might someday lose). To attenuate his portrait of d'Arnault, Jim introduced innuendoes of sexual incompetence. He recognizes d'Arnault's sensuality but impugns it by his image of sublimation: "all the agreeable sensations possible to creatures of flesh and blood were heaped up on those black-and-white keys, and he [was] gloating over them and trickling them through his yellow fingers." Jim's genteel opening phrase connotes male sexuality, which he must sublimate, displace from the man to the music, reduce to a *trickle*. D'Arnault "looks like some glistening African god of pleasure, full of strong, savage blood"; but superimposed is our familiar Uncle Tom "all grinning," "bowing to everyone, docile and happy."

Similarly, consider Jim's entrancing image of the four Danish girls who stand all day in the laundry ironing the townspeople's clothes. How charming they are: flushed and happy; how fatherly the laundryman offering water—no swollen ankles; no boredom or rancor; no exploitation: a cameo image from "the beautiful past." Peter and Pavel, dreadful to any ordinary mind for their murderous deed, ostracized by everyone, now disease-ridden and mindless, are to Jim picturesque outcasts: Pavel spitting blood; Peter spitting seeds as he desperately eats all his melons after kissing his cow goodbye, the only creature for him to love. And Mr. Shimerda's suicide. Jim reconciles himself to the horror of the mutilated body frozen in its own blood by imagining the spirit released and homeward bound to its beloved Bohemia. Only the evocative beauty of Cather's language—and the inevitable validation as childhood memory—can romanticize this sordid death and the squalor in which it takes place. Violence is as much the essence of prairie life as the growth of the wheat and blossoming of the corn. Violence appears suddenly and inexplicably, like the suicidal tramp. But Jim gives violence a cameo quality. He has the insistent need—and the strategy—to turn away from the very material he presents. He can forget the reaping-hook and reshape his dream. And as the novel reveals him doing this, it reveals our common usage of the past as a romance and refuge from the present. *My Ántonia* engraves a view of the past which is at best partial; at worst, blind. But our present is continuous with the whole past, as it was, despite Jim Burden's attempt to deny this, and despite Cather's "sad little refrain": "Our present is ruined—but we had a beautiful past." Beautiful to one who recreated it so; who desperately needed it so; who would deny the violence and the destructive attitudes toward race and sex immortalized in his very denial. We, however, have as desperate a need for clarity of vision as Jim had for nostalgia; and we must begin to look at *My Ántonia,* long considered a representatively American novel, not only for its beauty of art and for its affirmation of history, but also, and instructively, for its negations and evasions. Much as we would like to ignore them, for they bring painful confrontations, we must see what they would show us about ourselves—how we betray our past when we forget its most disquieting realities; how we begin to redeem it when we remember.

My Ántonia and the American Dream

James E. Miller, Jr.

Some books in our literature, like Walt Whitman's *Leaves of Grass* and Herman Melville's *Moby-Dick*, like F. Scott Fitzgerald's *The Great Gatsby* and Ernest Hemingway's *The Sun Also Rises,* assume a greater importance in our culture than their literary merit seems (at least at first glance) to justify. These are usually books that appear to reveal more about ourselves, our dreams, and our despairs than we had ever before recognized. Frequently these books are neglected on first appearance, or valued for reasons quite other than those that give them their later fame. It is quite possible that the authors wrote out of intense personal feeling and passion that had very little, at least on the conscious level, to do with the meanings we have come to recognize as the chief and enduring value of the books.

I would like to examine Willa Cather's *My Ántonia* as a book of this kind, offering perhaps an explanation for the way it often clings tenaciously in the mind, and even comes to haunt the reader long after he has put it down. Like the Fitzgerald and Hemingway novels, *My Ántonia* is, I believe, a commentary on the American experience, the American dream, and the American reality. It is the novel, after *Alexander's Bridge, O Pioneers!,* and *The Song of the Lark,* in which Willa Cather hit her stride in her own native material, and, in it, she penetrated more deeply, I think, into the dark recesses of the American psyche than in any of her later novels—though some of them might be more richly and complexly woven.

I would like to begin with an aspect of *My Ántonia* that helps burn it

From *Prairie Schooner* 48, no. 2 (Summer 1974). © 1974 by the University of Nebraska Press.

into the memory. Willa Cather in effect commented on the technique within the book, when she had Jim Burden say near the end, after his final visit to Ántonia on the Nebraska prairie: "Ántonia had always been one to leave images in the mind that did not fade—that grew stronger with time. In my memory there was a succession of such pictures, fixed there like the old woodcuts of one's first primer." It takes little imagination to transfer this statement to the novel itself, as we recall the strong and vivid images that it creates over and over again, usually in a few simple and seemingly effortless strokes.

One of these brilliant images stands in the heart of the book, and comes at the end of "The Hired Girls," the idyl placed near the end of book 2. That this episode represents also the emotional heart of the book is suggested by its derivation from the earlier 1909 story, "The Enchanted Bluff"—a story which, as Mildred Bennett has pointed out in her introduction to *Willa Cather's Collected Short Fiction, 1892–1912,* filters with emotional intensity through much of Cather's fiction. Jim Burden and the girls have spent the day out on the embankment of the prairie river, and as they seat themselves on a height overlooking the lands that have both threatened and succored them, they begin to talk about the future and the past. They fall slowly silent: "The breeze sank to stillness. In the ravine a ringdove mourned plaintively, and somewhere off in the bushes an owl hooted." Gradually the land itself becomes transfigured before their very eyes:

> Presently we saw a curious thing: There were no clouds, the sun was going down in a limpid, gold-washed sky. Just as the lower edge of the red disk rested on the high fields against the horizon, a great black figure suddenly appeared on the face of the sun. We sprang to our feet, straining our eyes toward it. In a moment we realized what it was. On some upland farm, a plough had been left standing in the field. The sun was sinking just behind it. Magnified across the distance by the horizontal light, it stood out against the sun, was exactly contained within the circle of the disk; the handles, the tongue, the share—black against the molten red. There it was, heroic in size, a picture writing on the sun.
>
> Even while we whispered about it, our vision disappeared; the ball dropped and dropped until the red tip went beneath the earth. The fields below us were dark, the sky was growing pale, and that forgotten plough had sunk back to its own little-ness somewhere on the prairie.

Most readers of *My Ántonia* have that black plow silhouetted against the red sun deeply etched in their minds. And they are likely to remember its heroic size and its hieroglyphic nature as a "picture writing on the sun"—as though left by some primitive race of giants who lived long ago in a heroic age and left their enigmatic mark and their obscure meaning in a scrawl on the heavenly body that served as their deity. But you will have noticed that I have quoted the paragraph that follows this vivid and suggestive imagery, describing simply the disappearance of the "vision." The plow that was a moment before so heroic and full of hidden meaning suddenly sinks back "to its own littleness somewhere on the prairie," and becomes "forgotten."

Too often, I suspect, we remember only that hieroglyphic plow etched into the sun, and forget Willa Cather's description of its swift shrinkage and disappearance, both from sight and from memory. In these succeeding images, we are, I want to suggest, near the heart not only of the book but of its hieroglyphic meaning. The novel is, in some sense, about a national experience—the frontier or pioneer experience—and its rapid diminishment and disappearance from the national memory. But more than an experience is involved and at stake. Obscurely related to the experience and its consequences is the American dream. Was it a trivial or mistaken impulse all along, magnified in the imagination beyond its possibilities? Was it a reality that was in some blundering way betrayed by us all? Or was it, perhaps, an illusion, created out of nothing, and, finally, disappearing into nothing, and well forgotten. I do not want to suggest that *My Ántonia* provides precise answers for these questions, inasmuch as it is a novel and not a tract. But I do want to indicate that the novel evokes these questions and explores them dramatically, leaving the reader to struggle with his own answers.

The image of the plow, first magnified and then shrunken and then obliterated, may stand as a paradigm for a recurrent pattern in *My Ántonia,* embodied most strikingly in the narrator, Jim Burden. For Jim the book might be described as a search for that lost and forgotten plow, or better perhaps, a quest for understanding the experience that caused the plow to magnify into a brilliant presence, and then to fade into insignificance and triviality. In brief, Jim is in search of the American past, his past, in an attempt to determine what went wrong, and perhaps as well what was right, with the dream. His is an attempt to read that "picture writing on the sun," and unravel the reasons for his own, and his country's anguished sense of loss. His loss is personal, because he, like the plow, once glowed in the sun and felt the expansion of life within him, life with all its promise and possibilities. But by the time we encounter him as the nostalgic narrator of *My Ántonia,* his life has diminished and faded, and he himself seems to feel the dark descend.

But of course no one with the name of Jim Burden could be a totally *un*allegorical figure. He carries with him not only his acute sense of personal loss but also a deep sense of national unease, a *burden* of guilt for having missed a chance, for having passed up an opportunity, for having watched with apathy as the dream dissipated in the rapidly disappearing past. The social burden may be all the heavier for Jim Burden because he has assigned himself the task of spokesman in the quest for what went wrong, or, better, what was missed, at a crucial moment of the national history. With him as the narrator of the book, we find out nearly everything about his past, but almost nothing about his present. The novel's "Introduction" provides one glimpse into his current unhappy state, given by his longtime friend and fellow Nebraskan:

> Although Jim Burden and I both live in New York, I do not see much of him there. He is legal counsel for one of the great Western railways and is often away from his office for weeks together. That is one reason why we seldom meet. Another is that I do not like his wife. She is handsome, energetic, executive, but to me she seems unimpressionable and temperamentally incapable of enthusiasm. Her husband's quiet tastes irritate her, I think, and she finds it worth while to play the patroness to a group of young poets and painters of advanced ideas and mediocre ability. She has her own fortune and lives her own life. For some reason, she wishes to remain Mrs. James Burden.

Although the glimpse is brief, it is sufficient to reveal an empty marriage, an artificial, even superficial, and trivialized life. Mrs. James Burden is destined to remain a shadowy character throughout the novel, but even so an important if only hovering presence, contrasting sharply in her vacuous super-sophistication with the women of the novel's action, and particularly with Jim's—or "my"—Ántonia. For it is she, the writer of the "Introduction" tells us, who has come to mean "the country, the conditions, the whole adventure" of their childhood. Thus as Jim recreates the story of his and, in part, the country's past, he envisions it through the disillusion of his—and, in part, his country's—unhappy present. It is, perhaps, only such disillusionment that enables Jim to recount the past without falsifying the brutalizing nature of the pioneer experience. All the first book of *My Ántonia,* entitled "The Shimerdas," is filled with animal imagery which suggests the diminishment of the lives of the people who have left their countries, their civilizations, their cultures behind and who have been reduced to confronting a hostile environment much as the animals confront it, scratching and scrabbling for the barest necessities of life itself. If the plow silhouetted against the sun somehow encompasses the free and open spirit embodied in Ántonia, it must be remembered that that plow also was the lure and background that ended in the suicide of old Mr. Shimerda and which turned Mrs. Shimerda into an envious scold and soured Ántonia's brother, Ambrosch, into a sullen sneak and brute. Many other lesser characters were demeaned and hardened by their cruel experiences. The entire first part of *My Ántonia* is remarkable for nostalgically evoking the past without blurring its harshness and its brutalizing weight. Ántonia is thus all the more remarkable for preserving her free and generous spirit in the face of all the crushing blows of the virgin prairie experience.

Thus *My Ántonia* does not portray, in any meaningful sense, the fulfillment of the American dream. By and large, the dreams of the pioneers lie shattered, their lives broken by the hardness of wilderness life. Even those who achieve, after long struggle, some kind of secure life are diminished in the genuine stuff of life. For example, in one of his accounts that reach into the future beyond the present action, Jim Burden tells us of the eventual fate of the vivacious Tiny Soderball, one of the few to achieve "solid worldly success." She had a series of exciting adventures in Alaska, ending up with a large fortune. But later, when Jim encountered her in Salt Lake City, she was a "thin, hard-faced woman. . . . She was satisfied with her success, but not elated. She was like someone in whom the faculty of becoming interested is worn out."

One of the major material successes of the book is Jim Burden, and in many ways the novel traces his rise in position and wealth. As most of the characters of the book travel west, his is a journey east, and, in the process, the acquisition of education, wealth, social position. In short, Jim has all the appearances of one who has lived the American dream and achieved fulfillment. But the material fulfillment has not brought the happiness promised. The entire novel is suffused with his melancholy at the loss of something precious—something that existed back in the hard times, now lost amidst comfort and wealth. The whole promise of the dream has somehow slipped through his fingers right at the moment it appeared within his grasp. Why? The question brings us around to a central problem in the novel: Why has Jim, so appreciative of the vitality and freedom represented by the hired girls, ended up in a marriage so empty of meaning?

Perhaps Jim's melancholy itself tells us the reason. The book in a way represents his confession, a confession of unaware betrayal of the dream. In looking back from his vantage point in time, Jim can come to the full realization of what the hired girls (especially such as Ántonia Shimerda and Lena Lingard) represented and what they have come to symbolize: simply all that is best, all that survives of worth, of the faded dream. Some critics have seen in Jim's obtuseness in his male–female relationship with Ántonia and Lena a defect in the book's construction. On the contrary, this theme is very much a part of the book's intention. Jim looking back from the wisdom of his later years and the unhappiness of his meaningless marriage can come to a much sharper awareness of precisely what he missed in his ambitious movement eastward and upward.

In book 2, "The Hired Girls," we are in a way witness to the dream turning sour: "The daughters of Black Hawk merchants had a confident, unenquiring belief that they were 'refined,' and that the country girls, who 'worked out,' were not." "The country girls were considered a menace to the social order. Their beauty shone out too boldly against a conventional background. But anxious mothers need have felt no alarm. They mistook the mettle of their sons. The respect for respectability was stronger than any desire in Black Hawk youth." Jim Burden remembered his roaming the streets of Black Hawk at night, looking at the "sleeping houses."

> for all their frailness, how much jealousy and envy and unhap-
> piness some of them managed to contain! The life that went on
> in them seemed to me made up of evasions and negations; shifts
> to save cooking, to save washing and cleaning, devices to pro-
> pitiate the tongue of gossip. This guarded mode of existence
> was like living under a tyranny. People's speech, their voices,
> their very glances, became furtive and repressed. Every individ-
> ual taste, every natural appetite, was bridled by caution.

"Respect for respectability" is, perhaps, the cancer battening at the heart of the dream (a theme that William Faulkner was to emphasize later in his Snopes trilogy), and the reader may wonder to what extent Jim Burden himself had been infected, especially in view of the brittle wife he had acquired at some stage in his rise to the top. Moreover, Jim was strongly attracted to the vitality of the hired girls, consciously and unconsciously, as revealed in a recurring dream he had:

> One dream I dreamed a great many times, and it was always
> the same. I was in a harvest-field full of shocks, and I was lying
> against one of them. Lena Lingard came across the stubble
> barefoot, in a short skirt, with a curved reaping-hook in her

hand, and she was flushed like the dawn, with a kind of luminous rosiness all about her. She sat down beside me, turned to me with a soft sigh and said, "Now they are all gone, and I can kiss you as much as I like."

After this remarkable sexual revelation, Jim adds: "I used to wish I could have this flattering dream about Ántonia, but I never did." Sister-like Ántonia cannot be transfigured, even in dream, to sexual figure. Her role in the book, and in Jim's psyche, is destined to be more idealized, more mythic.

But Lena Lingard is the subject of an entire book of *My Ántonia*. And that book works out metaphorically the meaning of the novel's epigraph from Virgil as well as the specific personal relation of Jim and Lena, this latter through symbolic use of a play they both attend, Dumas's *Camille*. The epigraph for *My Ántonia* is drawn from Virgil's *Georgics,* and reads: *"Optima dies . . . prima fugit."* This phrase comes into the novel in book 3, after Jim has entered the University of Nebraska and begun his study of Latin, translating the phrase "the best days are the first to flee." As Lena Lingard, now with a dressmaking shop in Lincoln, brings to mind for Jim all the vitality of the hired girls of Black Hawk, he makes the connection between them and the haunting phrase from Virgil: "It came over me, as it had never done before, the relation between girls like those and the poetry of Virgil. If there were no girls like them in the world, there would be no poetry. I understand that clearly, for the first time. This revelation seemed to me inestimably precious. I clung to it as if it might suddenly vanish."

But if Lena (along with Ántonia and the others) is equated with poetry, she is also a breathing physical reality to Jim, and book 3 brings Jim as close physically to one of the hired girls as the novel permits. A large part of the book is taken up with a description of Jim's and Lena's attendance at a performance of *Camille,* the sentimental but highly effective drama by Dumas *fils*. As Jim remarks: "A couple of jack-rabbits, run in off the prairie, could not have been more innocent of what awaited them than were Lena and I." Although some critics see the long account of theatre going as a kind of inserted story or intrusion, in fact it provides a kind of sophisticated mirror image in literature for the thematic dilemma posed in the novel itself—and particularly the dilemma Jim faces in his attraction to Lena. Only a few pages before this episode, he has come to the insight equating the hired girls, in all their vitality and freedom, with poetry. Now he is confronted with the physical presence of one for whom he feels a strong attraction.

The hired girls are not, of course, Camilles, but they have some of the same kind of magic, poetry, freedom, love of life that attracted Armand to Camille—and that attracts Jim to Lena. As Jim and Lena find themselves drawn closer and closer together in Lincoln, their conversation turns more and more to marriage—but only obliquely do they hint of anything deeper than friendship between themselves. Lena, pressed by Jim about her future, says she will never marry, that she prefers to be "lonesome," that the experience of marriage as she has witnessed it is even repellent. Jim answers, " 'But it's not all like that.' " Lena replies: " 'Near enough. It's all being under somebody's thumb. What's on your mind, Jim? Are you afraid I'll want you to marry me some day?' " Jim's immediate remark after this, to the reader, is: "Then I told her I was going away." The moment has passed, the future for Jim has been, in a sense, determined. Lena will go on her successful, "lonesome" way; Jim will go on to his considerable achievement and position—and his disastrous marriage.

What happened to the dream—to Jim's dream of Lena, to the larger dream of personal fulfillment? Was his failure in not seeing some connection between the dreams? Was Jim's destiny in some obscure sense a self-betrayal? And is this America's destiny, a self-betrayal of the possibilities of the dream? There are many literary texts that could be cited for parallels, but I want to limit myself to two that will, I hope, prove suggestive. The first is F. Scott Fitzgerald's novel, *The Great Gatsby*. There is, of course, a wide gulf between Jay Gatsby and Jim Burden (and in many ways Jim's function more nearly parallels Nick Carroway's), but Gatsby and Burden share in common a profound innocence and also, perhaps, a colossal illusion, a dream. And within themselves they carry the seeds of their own disaster or defeat. Gatsby's Daisy is not worthy of his dream, while Jim's Ántonia is perhaps worth more than his: but the point to be made is that both women are transfigured in the imagination to mythic dimensions, and become embodiments of the dream that is somehow, in the progress of both fictions, betrayed. At the end of *The Great Gatsby*, Nick Carroway sits on Gatsby's lawn meditating on Gatsby's life and death. In the deepening darkness he envisions the place as it must have looked to the first explorers and settlers: "Its vanished trees, the trees that had made way for Gatsby's house, had once pandered in whispers to the last and greatest of all human dreams; for a transitory enchanted moment man must have held his breath in the presence of this continent, compelled into an aesthetic contemplation he neither understood nor desired, face to face for the last time in history with something commensurate to his capacity for wonder." The problem with Gatsby, Nick realizes, is that he did not know that his dream "was already behind him, somewhere back in that vast obscurity beyond the city, where the dark fields of the republic rolled on under the night."

William Carlos Williams's *Paterson* is, as an epic poem, far different in structure and effect from either *My Ántonia* or *The Great Gatsby*. But thematically it touches on some of the same vital matters. The protagonist of the poem is in search throughout for *Beautiful Thing,* whether in the historical Paterson, New Jersey, or in the modern industrial city that shows all the signs of the contemporary wasteland. Only gradually does the reader come to realize that the search for Beautiful Thing is destined—probably—to be futile, because it has disappeared with the very past itself. A full understanding of the poem and the phrase will carry the reader back to Williams's earlier book, *In the American Grain,* and his inclusion of one of Columbus's accounts of his discovery of the New World. The account ends: "On shore I sent the people for water, some with arms, and others with casks; and as it was some little distance, I waited two hours for them. During that time I walked among the trees which was the most *beautiful thing* which I had ever seen." This same short passage is quoted by Williams some twenty-five years later, in *Paterson.* The protagonist of *Paterson* is in quest of that lost promise of the New World which Columbus found in the wilderness—among the trees—some centuries before.

Early in my discussion, I described one of Willa Cather's basic techniques as imagistic, and cited the example of the plow that stands out sharply etched and then disappears. Such images cluster near the end of *My Ántonia,* one of them characterizing Ántonia herself—or rather Ántonia as transfigured by Jim Burden's imagination. When, after many years have passed, Jim pays Ántonia his final visit—in book 5, "Cuzak's Boys"—Ántonia takes Jim out to see her fruit cave, and there Jim witnesses all her children dash out of the cave: "a veritable explosion of life out of the dark cave into the sunlight." This image of affirmation and vitality remains with Jim as somehow symbolic of all that Ántonia stands for—and all that he himself has somehow missed.

But the final image to be etched on the mind of the reader comes at the end of the book, as Jim wanders over the prairie after his final parting from Ántonia. It is a "bit of the first road that went from Black Hawk out to the north country"; "this half-mile or so within the pasture fence was all that was left of that old road which used to run like a wild thing across the open prairie." Jim begins to follow the road as far as he can:

> On the level land the tracks had almost disappeared—were mere shadings in the grass, and a stranger would not have noticed them. But wherever the road had crossed a draw, it was

easy to find. The rains had made channels of the wheelruts and washed them so deeply that the sod had never healed over them. They looked like gashes torn by a grizzly's claws, on the slopes where the farm-wagons used to lurch up out of the hollows with a pull that brought curling muscles on the smooth hips of the horses. I sat down and watched the haystacks turn rosy in the slanting sunlight.

This road is not, of course, simply Jim's and Ántonia's road. It is America's road, leading not into the future, but into the past, fast fading from the landscape, fast fading from memory. Like Gatsby's dream that lies somewhere out there already lost in the vastness of the continent, like *Paterson's* Beautiful Thing that appeared only for a brief moment as Columbus walked among the New World trees—the road beckons but eludes simultaneously. It is Jim's and Ántonia's—and perhaps America's—"road of Destiny":

> This was the road over which Ántonia and I came on that night when we got off the train at Black Hawk and were bedded down in the straw, wondering children, being taken we knew not whither. I had only to close my eyes to hear the rumbling of the wagons in the dark, and to be again overcome by that obliterating strangeness. The feelings of that night were so near that I could reach out and touch them with my hand. I had the sense of coming home to myself, and of having found out what a little circle man's experience is. For Ántonia and for me, this had been the road of Destiny; had taken us to those early accidents of fortune which predetermined for us all that we can ever be. Now I understood that the same road was to bring us together again. Whatever we had missed, we possessed together the precious, the incommunicable past.

As Americans who have dreamed the dream, we might say with Jim: "Whatever we have missed, we possess together the precious, the incommunicable past." In some dark sense, Jim's experience is the American experience, his melancholy sense of loss also his country's, his longing for something missed in the past a national longing.

The lost promise, the misplaced vision, is America's loss—our loss— and it haunts us all, still.

The Mysteries of Ántonia

Evelyn Helmick

Many scenes in the novels of Willa Cather generate a power of response in the reader that can hardly be explained by the events or the characters. Frequently the explanation for her ability to evoke such strong responses is the conscious connection of her art with the eternal themes of myth. Her concern with human problems was seldom contemporaneous, but, in her words, "slid back into yesterday's seven thousand years." At such times, her always beautifully crafted prose becomes mysticism; then it is at its greatest. One such scene, apparently simple in its actions and characterizations, but in fact complex in its simultaneous presentation of daily existence on the Nebraska frontier and of one of the oldest fertility rituals known to Western man, is the final book of *My Ántonia*. That book, "Cuzak's Boys," recreates in both meaning and structure the Eleusinian Mysteries observed by the Greeks before the eighth century B.C., probably by the Mycenaeans before them and by the Roman emperors long after.

The final book of the novel is not the only one for which Willa Cather provided a mythic background. One of the more obvious instances is the picture of Lena Lingard as a luminous white creature whom Jim Burden dreams of as a fertility goddess. Other echoes of earlier female divinities include the three Marys, reminiscent of the Bachantes, with their love for the spring dancing festivals and their involvement in stories of scandalous sexual behavior. The Dionysian theme is continued by the arrival of blind d'Arnault, who looked like "some glistening African god of pleasure, full

From *The Midwest Quarterly* 17, no. 2 (January 1976). © 1976 by *The Midwest Quarterly*.

of strong savage blood," and realizes a music that is barbarous and true, transferring his excitement to his listeners. The music of the black god and the dancing of the white goddesses make the "Hired Girls" chapter a rhapsody to man's instinctive urge for pleasure.

A less joyous primitive idea, the need for human sacrifice, recurs throughout the book. The first sacrifice must be, as it is in the earlier Cather novel of the frontier, *O Pioneers!,* that of the European father, in order to allow the female rule so prominent in agricultural society. His death in winter—again like John Bergson's of the preceding novel—is related to that ritual in which a corn goddess mourns for a dead loved one representing the vegetation. As Ántonia thinks of her father's death, she sees a "red streak of dying light, over the dark prairie." Again the "empty darkness," the "utter darkness" of a matriarchal world returns. Two other stories of sacrifice occur in this novel. One—*called* a sacrifice by Willa Cather—is told by Peter and Pavel, the bachelor brothers. In their youth in Russia, while driving a wedding party one night in a sleigh overtaken by wolves, they decided to throw the bride out to lighten the load. Always after that incident they were known as the two men who had fed the bride to the wolves. Occurring as it does in Russia, the rejection of the woman shows the contrast of her role in the Old World with the vital role she plays in the New. The religious significance, too, is apparent afterwards:

> the first thing either of them noticed was a new sound that
> broke into the clear air, louder than they had ever heard it be-
> fore—the bell of the monastery of their own village, ringing for
> early prayers.

The other sacrifice has as its basis the ancient summer fertility rites. The tramp who throws himself into the threshing machine on the hottest day of the summer is a substitute for the human whose body is dismembered and scattered through the fields to insure the next year's crops; in a female-dominated world, the sacrifice will naturally be male. A glance at the chapter on dying and reviving gods in *The Golden Bough* shows how widespread this custom was in early civilizations.

The mythic and ritualistic themes of *My Ántonia* are the prelude to the reenactment of the rites of Eleusis in book 5 of the novel. Earlier scenes foreshadow Ántonia's representation of the Great Mother archetype, that "human representation of the divine," who, Jung says, founded a culture. That she represents almost allegorically the very early Western frontier is most clearly seen when Jim thinks, "It is no wonder that her sons stood tall and straight. She was a rich mine of life, like the founders of early races." On the psychological level, her meaning is yet more explicit: "She lent herself to immemorial human attitudes which we recognize as universal and true." And further, she has religious import—the ability to reveal the meaning of everyday life. On all these levels, it is Ántonia's relation to the land that invests her with significance.

The earth goddess motif builds in *My Ántonia* to those rituals of the final chapter through parallels between Ántonia's story and Persephone's, beginning with the ritual of the "marriage of death." Ántonia's abortive alliance with Larry Donovan, her reunion with her mother, the birth of her child, her later fecundity all connect her story with the ancient myth. That story, recounted in the Homeric "Hymn to Demeter," assigned to the seventh century B.C., tells of the corn goddess who, having lost her daughter Persephone to the god of the underworld, wanders through the land carrying a torch in search of her. During the time of the search, her gift of fertility is withheld from the earth, threatening famine. At Eleusis, disguised as an old woman, Demeter commands the people to build her a sanctuary where she can conduct the rites of her mysteries of fertility and immortality. The threat of drought and famine is dispelled as Zeus arranges for Persephone to spend two-thirds of her time on earth with her mother, one-third in the underworld.

On this myth, or rather these several myths, were based the primitive rites of the Eleusinian Mysteries which were celebrated in the ancient world for perhaps two thousand years. What occurred precisely at Eleusis may never be known; through the centuries the initiates of the cult seem to have taken seriously the rites as mysteries. But from many sources, among them Plato's *Phaedrus*, Aristophanes' *The Frogs,* and works of Herodotus, Aristotle, Apuleius, and many others, as well as archeological discoveries, scholars have reconstructed a sequence of events that took place during the celebration. Descriptions of the rituals vary slightly, but the basic pattern remains constant in most studies. One of the earliest is Andrew Lang's account in his introduction to the 1899 translation of the *Homeric Hymns.* In his version the fertility goddess sits in her winter retreat below the earth where she is the "ruler of men outworn." The festival in her honor, according to Lang, includes many rites: a mystery play on the sacred legend, fastings, vigils, sacrifices, sacred objects displayed, sacred words uttered. This outline, although very general, finds agreement among nearly all authors who describe the ritual.

All agree that the Eleusinian Mysteries were celebrated in an agrarian festival on the Rarian plain honoring the goddess of fertility. First in the sequence came the Lesser Mysteries at Agrai in the spring to tell the story of Persephone's abduction and to celebrate her return from the underworld, preliminary instruction for the initiates in the knowledge to be imparted at the principal ritual in the fall. According to C. H. Moore in *The Religious Thought of the Greeks,* such preparation is at the very core of the ritual: "Mystery in the Greek sense is a ritual to which only those may be admitted who have first been prepared by some rites of purification or probation." Thus qualified, the initiates were ready to participate in the Greater Mysteries during the month of Boedromion, corresponding to our September and the beginning of October, the time of autumnal sowing in Greece. On the nineteenth the neophytes, or *mystae,* were led in a lengthy procession along the sacred way to Eleusis. There the first event after their arrival was the sacrifice of a pig, which was later buried in a subterranean chasm. The *mystae* then entered the *telestrion,* the sanctuary of Demeter, where in darkness and in complete silence they witnessed the sacred rites.

The ritual proper, as far as it can be reconstructed, consisted of several parts, all mystical performances celebrating the "religion of nature," which to the early Greeks demonstrated the unity of man's life with the vegetative world. One segment was the *legomena,* a kind of discourse whose chief purpose was to announce the birth of a divine child. Short liturgical statements or symbolic utterances may have been included. Although it is not always possible to distinguish the second segment, the *dromena,* from the whole of the ritual, its function was dramatic—the presentation of a pageant depicting symbolically events in the lives of Demeter and Persephone. At the close of this part of the initiation, a door was opened to reveal the *anaktoron,* the smaller room within the *telestrion* where objects sacred to the goddesses were stored. This part of the ritual, called the *deiknymena,* was conducted in total silence on the part of both the *mystae* and those representing the deities. Only when all these preceding devotions had been observed could the *mystae* enter into the *epopteia,* the highest state of initiation, again a revelation in silence—the reaping of an ear of corn in a blaze of light, according to Hippolytus, the writer of the early Christian era. Following this most sacred core of the rites, the votaries emerged to complete the long celebration with song and dance, further torchlight processions, and a sacramental meal.

The meanings of this symbolism seem rather obscure even to those scholars willing to grope for them. Aside from a vague idea of the identity of the human soul with the natural cycle of the seasons, little of the significance of the mysteries has been explained. Erwin Rohde attempts some explanation in *Psyche: The Cult of Souls and Belief in Immortality among the Greeks:*

In some way or other the *Mystae* must have had revealed to them the real meaning of the "nature-symbolism" hidden in the mystical performances. Witnessing these performances they are supposed to have learnt that the fate of the seed of corn, represented by Persephone, its disappearance beneath the earth and eventual rebirth, is an image of the fate of the human soul, which also disappears that it may live again. This, then, must be the real content of the holy Mystery.

But even Rohde agrees that this is only the vaguest of generalities. Although the poets may have hinted at the events of initiations and archeologists may have reconstructed many of the rites in their physical surroundings, the meanings of the mysteries at Eleusis seem to have been kept a secret indeed.

And yet to recognize that epiphany undergone by Jim Burden in the final scenes of *My Ántonia* is to realize that this kind of religious experience cannot be articulated. Of primary importance is the fact that the Eleusinian Mysteries are primordial matriarchal mysteries, and as such differ in purpose and structure from patriarchal mysteries more familiar to modern man. As Erich Neumann comments in his *Armor and Psyche: The Psychic Development of the Feminine:*

> The masculine mystery is bound up with the active heroic struggle of the ego and based on the central insight that "I and the father are one." But the primordial feminine mysteries have a different structure. They are mysteries of birth and rebirth and appear predominantly in three different forms: as birth of the *logos,* son of light; as birth of the daughter, the new self; and as birth of the dead in rebirth. Wherever we find this elementary feminine sybolism, we have—psychologically speaking—matriarchial mysteries, regardless of whether those initiated are men or women.

The matriarchal mysteries will start, as he says, from the priority of the phenomenal "material world" and thus will be chthonian. As feminine mysteries they will depend more on intuitive faculties and less on the rational and communicable. Jim's final thought in *My Ántonia* reflects his experience: "Whatever we had missed, we possessed together the precious, the incommunicable past." And as it is throughout the novel, his own past is clearly related to the racial past. His initiation demonstrates to him that only through Ántonia and the symbols surrounding her can he understand an important part of his world; but just what he understands is too large to be precisely articulated. He can only say of Ántonia, she still had that something which fires the imagination, could still stop one's breath for a moment by a look or gesture that somehow revealed the meaning of common things. She had only to stand in the orchard, to put her hand on a little crab tree and look up at the apples, to make you feel the goodness of planting and tending and harvesting at last.

However penumbral this may be, it is undeniable that Jim experiences a spiritual transformation and that the mystical depth of his experience has great impact on the reader. Together, Jim and the reader have been initiated into the matriarchal mysteries of Eleusis.

Jim's initiation begins, properly enough, with instruction to prepare him for the principal ritual. Here, the "Lesser Mysteries" are imparted during his visit to the Widow Steavens where she tells him of Ántonia's "marriage of death." Even as he approaches her farm, his observations are filled with images of fertility appropriate to the maternal mysteries. The link with the classical era when those mysteries were celebrated is provided by his reference to Mrs. Steavens' massive head, so like a Roman senator's, and the ritualistic setting is sketched as Mrs. Steavens places a lamp in a corner of the room and turns it low, then sits formally in her rocking chair to deliver her information. The ritual implications are explicit here: "She crossed her hands in her lap and sat as if she were at a meeting of some kind." She tells Jim of Ántonia's departure on a cold, raw night from Black Hawk to be the bride of a railroad conductor, who later runs to "Old Mexico"—Ántonia refers to it as "down there"—when he and his fellow conductors are described as evil men. Although the allusions are slight, they serve to identify Ántonia's would-be groom with the underworld and hence with the drama of Persephone. Ántonia returns during a lovely warm May, wearing the veils which often distinguish statues of the earth goddess in classical sculpture. The strongest echo of the Demeter-Persephone myth, however, is Mrs. Steavens' rather strangely worded comment at the end of the story: "Jimmy, I sat right down on that bank beside her and made lament." Here she is the mother Demeter mourning the abduction of her daughter, just as later Ántonia mourns the loss of her own daughter, even to a happy marriage: "I cried like I was putting her into her coffin." The cyclical pattern underlying the message of the mysteries is prominent in this episode, as in the whole of the novel.

Jim's preparation for the Greater Mysteries is completed when he visits Ántonia immediately after his conversation with Mrs. Steavens. The end of that meeting is marked by the light symbolism mentioned by nearly every writer who has described the events at Eleusis:

> In that singular light every little tree and shock of wheat, every
> sunflower stalk and clump of snow-on-the-mountain, drew it-
> self up high and pointed; the very clods and furrows in the
> fields seemed to stand up sharply. I felt the old pull of the earth,
> the solemn magic that comes out of those fields at nightfall.

As the sky darkens, Jim searches Ántonia's face, that "closest, realest face,
under all the shadows of women's faces, at the very bottom of my memory." In those phrases can be discovered the two important meanings of
the novel relating it to the Eleusinian Mysteries—the supremacy of woman
who is allied with nature and the depth of the racial memory.

The emphasis throughout the book is on Ántonia; as Willa Cather
told her friend Elizabeth Sergeant, she meant Ántonia to *be* the story. As
in other early Cather stories, the woman remains rooted in her country,
while the man travels; the woman is content with things of the earth,
while the man seeks intellectual activity; the woman finds spiritual fulfillment, while the man fails spiritually. The man, then, must be taught
the feminine secrets, just as we know he was initiated into the Greek mysteries. "Happy is he among men upon earth who has seen these mysteries," the Homeric "Hymn to Demeter" tells us. Man's experience at
Eleusis was, Erich Neumann says in *The Great Mother*, predominantly
emotional and unconscious as he "sought to identify himself with Demeter, i.e., with his own feminine aspect," or the *anima*, in Jungian terms.
In *My Ántonia* this identification actually takes place before the celebration
of the mysteries, during the first of the two visits Jim pays Ántonia. He
tells her,

> I'd have liked to have you for a sweetheart, or a wife, or my
> mother or my sister—anything that a woman can be to a man.
> The idea of you is a part of my mind; you influence my likes
> and dislikes, all my tastes, hundreds of times when I don't real-
> ize it. You really are a part of me.

And for Ántonia, Jim is, of course the masculine principle within, the *ani-
mus*. Even if he never returns, she tells him, he's there with her. During
this exchange, nature herself blends male and female principles: Jim recalls,

> As we walked homeward across the fields, the sun dropped and
> lay like a great golden globe in the low west. While it hung
> there, the moon rose in the east, as big as a car-wheel, pale sil-
> ver and streaked with rose colour, thin as a bubble or a ghost-
> moon. For five, perhaps ten minutes, the two luminaries con-
> fronted each other across the level land, resting on opposite
> edges of the world.

The awareness that each is irrefragably bound to the other is the most significant development of the informal preparation for the rites to follow.

Jim's visit to Ántonia and her family twenty years later repeats rather precisely the ceremony at Eleusis, as far as it is known. As he enters the grounds, two of Ántonia's sons are examining their dead dog, the equivalent of the animal sacrifice at Eleusis and a reminder that a ceremony of resurrection must include a recognition of death. The boys follow Jim's buggy solemnly to the house after opening the gate for him, another boy ties his team with a flourish and two girls welcome him into the house. Ántonia's appearance on the scene overwhelms Jim: "The miracle happened; one of those quiet moments that clutch the heart, and take more courage than the noisy, excited passages in life."

There follow in rapid succession the segments of the rituals at Eleusis. First the *legomena,* or discourse, takes the form of an introduction to Ántonia's children, especially to Leo, the favorite who represents the divine child, a view he himself apparently shares. His awareness of his "secret," his power of enjoyment, his intuitive recognitions, and most of all his animal-like appearance all point to him as one of those happy rural dieties of the classical era. (Ántonia's grandson, too, shares in her glory; although he is not divine, he is called "a little prince.") In the *legomena,* the liturgical element is merely suggested by Leo's well-rehearsed reply to his mother's question about his age and by the girls' response of "mother" in unison as Ántonia declares that she loves this child best. The second segment of the ceremony, the *dromena,* or dramatic reenactment, involves Leo, too. Beckoned by Ántonia, he fearfully tells her softly in Bohemian about the dead dog, while she soothes him. She later whispers to him a secret promise which he in turn whispers to his sister.

The next part of the ritual, the *dieknymena,* or display of sacred objects, becomes in the Nebraska version a descent to the fruit cave of the farm. Each child very proudly shows some of the barrels and jars of preserved food, maintaining the silence of the Eleusinian rites:

> Nína and Jan, and a little girl named Lucie, kept shyly pointing out to me the shelves of glass jars. They said nothing, but, glancing at me, traced on the glass with the fingertips the outline of the cherries and strawberries and crabapples within, trying by a blissful expression of countenance to give me some idea of their deliciousness.

The blissful expressions lead us to reflect that on the frontier such secrets held almost religious import; on their mastery depended the very survival of that civilization. In the course of the ritual, then Ántonia and Jim ascend the stairs of the cave first, and here Jim's revelation, the *epopteia,* begins. The children follow them:

> they all came running up the steps together, big and little, tow heads and gold heads, and brown, and flashing little naked legs; a veritable explosion of life out of the dark cave into the sunlight. It made me dizzy for a moment.

The identification of Ántonia's twelve children—it is impossible not to connect them with the divisions of the year and the vegetative world, particularly the sacred ears of corn—is complete at this point. As Jim later reflects on this experience, he says,

> That moment, when they all came tumbling out of the cave into the light, was a sight any man might have come far to see. Ántonia had always been one to leave images in the mind that did not fade—that grew stronger with time.

Even the transformation scene—that blaze of visible and intuitive light so prominent in the literature on the mysteries and the basis for the climax of the "Hymn to Demeter"—is included. In the hymn, before Demeter and her daughter vanish, "the bare leafless expanse of the Eleusinian plain is suddenly turned, at the will of the goddess, into a vast sheet of ruddy corn." In the novel Ántonia takes Jim through the orchard, where "the afternoon sun poured down on us through the drying grape leaves. The orchard seemed full of sun, like a cup." Every tree, every fruit, even the ducks reflect this light. As Ántonia tells of her life on the frontier, she looks through the orchard, "where the sunlight was growing more and more golden." Jim's initiation into "that mystery of mysteries which it is meet to call the most blessed" is consummated, then, as the skies shine their approval; there remains only the post-ceremonial merrymaking. At the feast, instead of the sacred cakes and *kykeon* of Eleusis, the celebrants dine on *kolaches* and milk. All eyes are excitedly on Ántonia during the dinner, and as afterwards, carrying the lamp, she leads the party into the parlor—a reenactment of the torchlight procession in the Greek festival— where the children provide the musical entertainment. To the very last event, the sequence of rites on the Cuzak farm has paralleled that of the Eleusinian Mysteries.

In her vision of early Nebraska Willa Cather has offered unsuspected meaning through those parallels between Eleusis and the frontier. Of even greater significance to the novel is the presentation of Ántonia as a goddesswoman—that female who is "no less a marvel than the universe itself," in Joseph Campbell's words. Both visions provide a dimension to the mythic meaning of the American past that few authors have equalled.

The Defeat of a Hero: Autonomy and Sexuality in *My Ántonia*

Deborah G. Lambert

My Ántonia (1918), Willa Cather's celebration of the American frontier experience, is marred by many strange flaws and omissions. It is, for instance, difficult to determine who is the novel's central character. If it is Ántonia, as we might reasonably assume, why does she entirely disappear for two of the novel's five books? If, on the other hand, we decide that Jim Burden, the narrator, is the central figure, we find that the novel explores neither his consciousness nor his development. Similarly, although the narrator overtly claims that the relationship between Ántonia and Jim is the heart of the matter, their friendship actually fades soon after childhood: between these two characters there is only, as E. K. Brown said, "an emptiness where the strongest emotion might have been expected to gather." Other inconsistencies and contradictions pervade the text—Cather's ambivalent treatment of Lena Lingard and Tiny Soderball, for example—and all are in some way related to sex roles and to sexuality.

This emphasis is not surprising: as a writer who was also a woman, Willa Cather faced the difficulties that confronted, and still do confront, accomplished and ambitious women. As a professional writer, Cather began, after a certain point in her career, to see the world and other women, including her own female characters, from a male point of view. Further, Cather was a lesbian who could not, or did not, acknowledge her homosexuality and who, in her fiction, transformed her emotional life and expe-

From *American Literature* 53, no. 4 (January 1982). © 1982 by Duke University Press.

riences into acceptable, heterosexual forms and guises. In her society it was difficult to be a woman and achieve professionally, and she could certainly not be a woman who loved women; she responded by denying, on the one hand, her womanhood and, on the other, her lesbianism. These painful denials are manifest in her fiction. After certain early work, in which she created strong and achieving women, like herself, she abandoned her female characters to the most conventional and traditional roles; analogously, she began to deny or distort the sexuality of her principal characters. *My Ántonia*, written at a time of great stress in her life, is a crucial and revealing work, for in it we can discern the consequences of Cather's dilemma as a lesbian writer in a patriarchal society.

I

Many, if not all, achieving women face the conflict between the traditional idea of what it is to be a woman and what it is to achieve. Achievement in most fields has been reserved for males; passivity—lack of assertiveness and energy, and consequent loss of possibility of achievement— has been traditionally female. When the unusual girl, or woman, rebels and overcomes the limitations imposed on women, she suffers from the anxiety produced by conflict. Although such a woman is, and knows she is sexually female, in her professional life she is neither female nor male. Finding herself in no-woman's land, she avoids additional anxiety by not identifying herself professionally as a woman or with other women. Carolyn Heilbrun, who diagnoses and prescribes for a variety of women's dilemmas, writes: "Sensing within themselves, as girls, a longing for accomplishment, they have, at great cost, with great pain, become honorary men, adopting at the same time, the general male attitude towards women."

From childhood, Willa Cather was determined to achieve and she perceived, correctly, that achieving in the world was a male prerogative. When she decided as a child to become a doctor, she also began to sign herself "William Cather, MD," or "Willie Cather, MD," and she pursued her vocation seriously, making house calls with two Red Cloud physicians, and on one occasion giving chloroform while one of them amputated a boy's leg. She also demonstrated her clear understanding of nineteenth-century sex roles and her preference for "male" activities when she entered in a friend's album two pages of "The Opinion, Tastes and Fancies of Wm. Cather, MD." In a list that might have been completed by Tom Sawyer, she cites "slicing toads" as a favorite summer occupation; doing fancy work as "real misery"; amputating limbs as "perfect happiness"; and dressing in skirts as "the greatest folly of the Nineteenth Century." At college in Lincoln, her appearance in boyishly short hair and starched shirts rather than the customary frilly blouses—like her desire to play only male roles in college dramatic productions—continued to reflect her "male" ambition. James Woodress, Cather's biographer, speaks of a "strong masculine element" in her personality, a phrase that may obscure what she saw clearly from childhood: that womanhood prohibited the achievement she passionately sought.

After some measure of professional success, Cather began to identify with her male professional peers, rather than with women. Her review of Kate Chopin's novel *The Awakening* (1899) is a poignant example of the troubling consequences of this identification. First, Cather describes Edna Pontellier's struggle towards identity as "trite and sordid" and then, comparing Edna to Emma Bovary, adds contemptuously that Edna and Emma "belong to a class, not large, but forever clamoring in our ears, that demands more out of life than God put into it." In a final irony, Cather writes of Chopin that "an author's choice of themes is frequently as inexplicable as his choice of a wife." Like Flaubert and other male authors with whom she identifies, Cather fails to understand, let alone view sympathetically, the anguish that Chopin brilliantly portrays in Edna's life and death.

Nevertheless, in two novels written before *My Ántonia*, she accomplished what few women authors have: the creation of strong, even heroic, women as protagonists. Cather succeeded in this because she could imagine women achieving identity and defining their own purposes. The woman author, whose struggle toward selfhood and achievement is marked by painful conflict, rarely reproduces her struggle in fiction, perhaps findings its recreation too anxiety-producing, or perhaps simply not being able to imagine the forms that a woman's initiation might take. George Eliot and Edith Wharton, to mention only two familiar examples, never created women characters who possessed their own intelligence, ambition, or autonomy. Characteristically, women authors transpose their own strivings to their male characters and portray women in conventional roles. (In this case, the roles ascribed to women in fiction are the same as those ascribed to them in society.) The occasional male author—E. M. Forster, James, and Hawthorne are examples—will create an independent, even heroic, female character, perhaps because male progress toward identity, demanded and supported by society, is generally a less anxious process.

Alexandra Bergson in *O Pioneers!* (1913) and Thea Kronberg in *The*

Song of the Lark (1915) are female heroes, women not primarily defined by relationship to men, or children, but by commitment to their own destinies and their own sense of themselves. Alexandra inherits her father's farm lands and grandfather's intelligence: although her father has two grown sons, he chooses Alexandra to continue his work, because she is the one best suited by nature to do so. Developing Nebraska farmland becomes Alexandra's mission, and she devotes herself to it unstintingly. She postpones marriage until she is nearly forty years old, and then marries Carl, the gentle and financially unsuccessful friend of her childhood. Ultimately, Alexandra has success, wealthy independence, and a marriage which, unlike passionate unions in Cather's fiction, will be satisfying rather than dangerous. In this portrait of Alexandra, Cather provides a paradigm of the autonomous woman, even while she acknowledges, through the images of Alexandra's fantasy lover, the temptations of self-abnegation and passivity.

Thea Kronberg dedicates herself to music, and her talent defines and directs her life. Born into a large frontier family, she clearsightedly pursues her goals, selecting as friends those few who support her aspirations. Subordinating personal life to the professional, Thea, like Alexandra, marries late in life, after she has achieved success; and her husband, too, recognizes and accepts her special mission. There is never a question of wooing either of these women away from their destinies to the conventional life of women. Marriage, coming later in life, after identity and achievement, is no threat to the self; moreover, Cather provides her heroines with sensitive, even androgynous, males who are supportive of female ambition. But Alexandra and Thea are unusual, imaginative creations primarily because they embody autonomy and achievement. In these books, Cather does not transpose her struggle for success to male characters, as women authors often have, but instead risks the creation of unusual female protagonists.

What Cather achieved in these two early novels she no longer achieved in her later works. Indeed she stopped portraying strong and successful women and began to depict patriarchal institutions and predominantly male characters. Although she wrote ten more novels, in none of them do we find women like Alexandra and Thea. *Death Comes for the Archbishop* (1927) and *Shadows on the Rock* (1931) are Cather's best-known late novels, and in the former there are virtually no women, while in the latter, women are relegated to minor and entirely traditional roles. Cather's movement toward the past in these novels—toward authority, permanence, and Rome—is also a movement into a world dominated by patriarchy. The writer who could envision an Alexandra and a Thea came to be a celebrant of male activity and institutions.

In this striking transformation, *My Ántonia* is the transitional novel. Given the profound anxieties that beset women authors when they recreate their search for selfhood in female characters, it is not surprising that Cather turned to a male narrative point of view. She rationalized that the omniscient point of view, which she had used in both *O Pioneers!* and *The Song of the Lark,* was not appropriate for her subject matter and continued to ignore the advice of Sarah Orne Jewett, who told her that when a woman tried to write from a man's point of view, she inevitably falsified. Adopting the male persona was, for Cather, as it has been for many other writers, a way out of facing great anxiety. Moreover, it is natural to see the world, and women, from the dominant perspective, when that is what the world reflects and literature records. Thus, in *My Ántonia,* for the first time in her mature work, Cather adopts a male persona, and that change marks her transition to fiction increasingly conventional in its depiction of human experience.

II

Cather was not only a woman struggling with the dilemma of the achieving woman: she was also a lesbian, and that, too, affected the fiction that she wrote. Early in life she had decided never to marry, and in reviews and letters she repeatedly stressed that marriage and the life of the artist were utterly incompatible. She seems always to have loved women: indeed her only passionate and enduring relationships were with women. Her first, and probably greatest, love was Isabel McClung, whom she met in Pittsburgh in 1898. Moving into the McClung family home, Cather lived there for five years and worked in a small room in the attic. There she wrote most of *April Twilights* (1903), her book of poems; *The Troll Garden* (1905), a short story collection; and major parts of *O Pioneers!* and *The Song of the Lark.* Her affair with McClung continued until 1916, when McClung suddenly announced that she was going to marry the violinist Jan Hambourg. At this point, Cather's world seems to have collapsed. She was first stunned and then deeply depressed. Her loss of McClung seems to have been the most painful event of her life, and it was six months before she could bring herself to see the couple. After a long visit to Red Cloud, and a shorter one to New Hampshire, she eventually returned to New York. There she took up her life with Edith Lewis, with whom she was to live for forty years in a relationship less passionate than that with

McClung. But clearly, throughout her life, Cather's deepest affections were given to women. During the troubled period when she felt abandoned by McClung, Cather was writing *My Ántonia:* both her sense of loss and the need to conceal her passion are evident in the text.

Cather never adequately dealt with her homosexuality in her fiction. In two early novels, the question of sexuality is peripheral: *Alexander's Bridge* (1912) and *The Song of the Lark* concern the integration of identity, and the expression of sexuality is limited and unobtrusive. Yet Cather began to approach the issue of homosexuality obliquely in subsequent novels. Many, although not all, of the later novels include homosexual relationships concealed in heterosexual guises. Joanna Russ points out that these disguised relationships are characterized by an irrational, hopeless quality and by the fact that the male member of the couple, who is also the central consciousness of the novel, is unconvincingly male—is, in fact, female and a lesbian. The relationships of Claude and Enid in *One of Ours* (1922) and Niel and Marian Forrester in *A Lost Lady* (1923) are cases in point. In *O Pioneers!,* the novel which preceded *My Ántonia,* the love story of Alexandra's brother Emil and Marie, is also such a transposed relationship: to consider its treatment is to notice, from another perspective, the significant changes that occurred in Cather's writing at the time of *My Ántonia.*

In the subplot of Emil and Marie's love, which unexpectedly dominates the second half of *O Pioneers!,* Cather implies the immense dangers of homosexual love. The deaths of Emil and Marie at the moment of sexual consummation suggest more than a prohibition against adultery: their story expresses both a fantasy of sexual fulfillment and the certainty that death is the retribution for this sort of passion. Seeing the story of Emil and Marie in this way, as the disguised expression of another kind of passion, becomes increasingly plausible when one examines Emil's character and behavior and observes that he is male in name only; moreover, it offers a convincing explanation for the sudden and shocking intrusion of violence in this otherwise uniformly elegiac novel. But what is most important here is that Alexandra, Cather's hero, is not destroyed by the consequences of Emil's passion; instead, passion vicariously satisfied, Alexandra retreats to the safety of heterosexual marriage. Thus the fantasy of homosexuality, and the fear of it, are encapsulated and controlled, only slightly distorting the narrative structure. Three years later, Cather's fear is pervasive and dominates the development of *My Ántonia,* so that the narrative structure itself becomes a defense against erotic expression.

The original of Ántonia was Annie Sadilek Pavelka, a Bohemian woman whom Cather had loved and admired from childhood, and with whom she maintained a lifelong, affectionate friendship. In 1921, after completion of the novel, Cather wrote of her feeling for Annie and her decision to use the male point of view:

> Of the people who interested me most as a child was the Bohemian hired girl of one of our neighbors, who was so good to me. . . . Annie fascinated me and I always had it in mind to write a story about her. . . . Finally, I concluded that I would write from the point of view of the detached observer, because that was what I had always been. Then I noticed that much of what I knew about Annie came from the talks I had with young men. She had a fascination for them, and they used to be with her whenever they could. They had to manage it on the sly, because she was only a hired girl. But they respected her, and she meant a good deal to some of them. So I decided to make my observer a young man.

Here Cather suggests the long genesis of this tale and, significantly, her own replication of the "male" response to Annie, reflected in the language of the passage: "Annie fascinated me"/"She had a fascination for them." The fascination here seems to imply not only a romantic and sexual attraction, but also horror at the attraction. Cather suggests that the young men's response to Ántonia is ambivalent because Annie is forbidden; she is a hired girl, with all of that phrase's various suggestions, and so they see her "on the sly." For Cather that fascination is more complex. Identifying with the young men in their forbidden response to Annie, her impulse is that of the lesbian. Yet, when she wrote the novel and transposed to Jim her own strong attraction to Annie/Ántonia, she also transposed her restrictions on its erotic content. Although she adopts the male persona, she cannot allow him full expression of her feelings. Thus, what would seem to be Jim's legitimate response to Ántonia is prohibited and omitted: its homosexual threat is, evidently, too great, and so we find at the heart of the novel that emptiness noted by Brown.

The avoidance of sexuality (which does not extend beyond the Jim-Ántonia relationship, however) must be seen in connection with McClung's desertion of Cather, which occurred after she had composed the first two or three chapters of *My Ántonia*. During this time of grieving, she seemed not to trust herself to write of her own experience of love and sex. For the Cather persona and the beloved woman are not only separated: both are actually denied sexuality, although sexuality arises in distorted, grotesque forms throughout the novel.

During the writing of *My Ántonia,* Cather's grief coincided with the already great burden of anxiety of the woman who is a writer. After this time, her heroic stance in her fiction could not continue, and she abandons the creation of strong fictional women. In *My Ántonia* she denies Jim's erotic impulses and Ántonia's sexuality as well; and she retreats into the safety of convention by ensconcing Ántonia in marriage and rendering her apotheosis as earth mother. She abandons Ántonia's selfhood along with her sexuality: as Mrs. Cuzak, Ántonia is "a battered woman," and a "rich mine of life, like the founders of early races." Interestingly, critics have recognized the absence of sexuality in Jim, although not in Ántonia, and focus their analyses on the male in the case, as though the novel had been written about a male character by a male author—or, as if the male experience were always central.

The most complex and instructive of the psychological analyses of Jim is by Blanche Gelfant, who sees Jim as a young man whose adolescence "confronts him with the possibility of danger in women." He cannot accept the "nexus of love and death," and so retreats to perpetual boyhood. Noting many of the novel's ambiguous elements, Gelfant assumes that male fragility and male fear of womanhood is the crux of the problem. In her view, Jim is the protagonist and Ántonia is his guide: she is responsible for his failed initiation and, later, for his sexual humiliation and confusion. Gelfant's analysis assumes traditional sex roles as normative: Jim's experience is central and Ántonia's is the subordinate, supporting role in his adventure. Yet, to understand the ambiguity in this, and perhaps in other texts by women writers, requires the reversal of such assumptions. If we assume the centrality of Ántonia and her development in the novel, we can observe the stages by which Cather reduces her to an utterly conventional and asexual character.

III

In childhood, Ántonia is established as the novel's center of energy and vitality. As a girl she is "bright as a new dollar" with skin "a glow of rich, dark colour" and hair that is "curly and wild-looking." She is always in motion: holding out a hand to Jim as she runs up a hill, chattering in Czech and broken English, asking rapid questions, struggling to become at home in a new environment. Wanting to learn everything, Ántonia also has "opinions about everything." Never indolent like Lena Lingard, or passive like her sister Yulka, or stolid like the Bohemian girls, Ántonia is "breathless and excited," generous, interested, and affectionate. By the end of her childhood, however, intimations of her future social roles appear.

When Ántonia reaches puberty, Cather carefully establishes her subordinate status in relation to three males, and these relationships make an interesting comparison with Alexandra's and Thea's. First, Ántonia's brutal brother, Ambrosch, is established as the head of the house and the "important person in the family." Then Jim records his need to relegate Ántonia to secondary status and receive deference, since "I was a boy and she was a girl," and in the farcical, pseudo-sexual snake-killing episode, he believes he accomplishes his goal. In fact, he and Ántonia enact a nearly parodic ritual of male and female behavior: in his fear, he turns on her with anger; she cries and apologizes for her screams, despite the fact that they may have saved his life; and she ultimately placates him with flattery. Forced to leave school, she soon relinquishes all personal goals in favor of serving others. No longer resentful or competitive, she is "fairly panting with eagerness to please" young Charley Harling, the son of her employers: "She loved to put up lunches for him when he went hunting, to mend his ball-gloves and sew buttons on his shooting coat, baked the kind of nut-cake he liked, and fed his setter dog when he was away on trips with his father." Cather's protagonist has been reduced to secondary status, as Alexandra and Thea were not: having challenged our expectations in earlier works, Cather retreats in this novel to the depiction of stereotypical patterns.

The second book of *My Ántonia,* with its insinuative title "The Hired Girls," dramatizes the emergence of Ántonia's intense sexuality and its catastrophic effects on her world. Now a beautiful adolescent woman, Ántonia is "lovely to see, with her eyes shining and her lips always a little parted when she danced. That constant dark colour in her cheeks never changed." Like flies the men begin to circle around her—the iceman, the delivery boys, the young farmers from the divide; and her employer, Mr. Harling, a demanding, intimidating, patriarch insists that she give up the dances where she attracts so much attention. When she refuses, he banishes her from his family. Next becoming the object of her new employer's lust, Ántonia loses Jim's affection and, by the end of the summer, has embarked on a disastrous affair with the railroad conductor, Donovan. Ántonia's sexuality is so powerful, in Cather's portrayal, that is destroys her oldest and best friendships and thrusts her entirely out of the social world of the novel.

Jim's intense anger at Ántonia once again reveals his fear, this time a fear of her sexuality that is almost horror. When Cutter attempts to rape her, Jim, the actual victim of the assault, returns battered to his grandmother's house. He then blames Ántonia and her sexuality for Cutter's lust, and recoils from her: "I heard Ántonia sobbing outside my door, but

I asked grandmother to send her away. I felt I never wanted to see her again. I hated her almost as much as I hated Cutter. She had let me in for all this disgustingness." This eruption of sexuality marks the climax, almost the end, of the friendship between Ántonia and Jim, and after this, Ántonia is virtually banished from the novel.

At this point, Cather, evidently retreating from the sexual issue, broadens the novel's thematic focus. Jim and Ántonia do not meet again for two years, and all of book 3 is devoted to Jim's frivolous, romanticized affair with Lena Lingard, with which he and the reader are diverted. Moreover, the events of Ántonia's life—her affair with Donovan, her pregnancy, her return home, the birth of her daughter—are kept at great narrative distance. Two years after the fact, a neighbor describes these events to Jim as she has seen them, or read about them in letters. Yet, as though banishing Ántonia and distracting Jim were not sufficient, her sexuality is diminished and then, finally, destroyed. After a punitive pregnancy and the requisite abandonment by her lover, she never again appears in sexual bloom. The metaphoric comparisons that surround her become sexually neutral, at best. In one example her neck is compared to "the bole of a tree," and her beauty is cloaked: "After the winter began she wore a man's long overcoat and boots and a man's felt hat with a wide brim." Her father's clothes, like Mr. Harling's ultimatum, seem well designed to keep Ántonia's sexuality under wraps.

After a two-year separation, during which Ántonia returns to her brother's farm, bears her child, and takes up her life of field work, Jim and Ántonia meet briefly. Dreamlike and remote, their meeting is replete with nostalgia not readily accounted for by events; as Jim says, "We met like people in the old song, in silence, if not in tears." Inappropriately, though in a speech of great feeling, Ántonia compares her feeling for Jim to her memory of her father, who is lost to her for reasons that the text does provide:

> you are going away from us for good. . . . But that don't mean I'll lose you. Look at my papa here, he's been dead all these years, and yet he is more real to me than almost anybody else. He never goes out of my life.

Jim's response expresses similar nostalgia and an amorphous yearning:

> since I've been away, I think of you more often than of anyone else in this part of the world. I'd have liked to have you for a sweetheart, or a wife, or my mother, or my grandmother, or my sister—anything that a woman can be to a man. . . . You really are a part of me.

The seductive note of sentiment may blind us as readers to the fact that Jim might offer to marry Ántonia and instead abandons her to a life of hardship on her brother's farm with an empty, and ultimately broken promise to return soon. Cather forcibly separates Jim and Ántonia because of no logic given in the text; we have to assume that her own emotional dilemma affected the narrative and to look for the reasons within Cather herself.

Following this encounter is a twenty-year hiatus: when Jim and Ántonia finally meet again, the tensions that have lain behind the novel are resolved. Ántonia, now devoid of sexual appeal, no longer presents any threat. In addition, she has been reduced to a figure of the greatest conventionality: she has become the stereotypical earth mother. Bearing no resemblance to Cather's early female heroes, she is honored by Jim and celebrated by Cather as the mother of sons. By the novel's conclusion, Cather has capitulated to a version of that syndrome in which the unusual, achieving woman recommends to other women as their privilege and destiny that which she herself avoided. While recognizing the conflict that issues in such self-betrayal, one also notes the irony of Cather's glorification of Ántonia.

Autonomy and unconventional destiny are available only to the subordinate characters, Lena Lingard and Tiny Soderball, two of the hired girls. Lena, having seen too much of marriage, childbearing and poverty, has established a successful dressmaking business and, despite her sensuous beauty, refrained from marriage. Her companion, Tiny, made her fortune in the Klondike before settling down in San Francisco. They lived in a mutually beneficial, supportive relationship: "Tiny audits Lena's accounts occasionally and invests her money for her; and Lena, apparently, takes care that Tiny doesn't grow too miserly," Jim tells us. Both Lena and Tiny are independent and unconventional; Lena particularly understands and values the single self. In a revealing detail, she instructs her brother to buy handkerchiefs for her mother with an embroidered "B" for her given name, "Berthe," rather than with an "M" for mother. Lena, who describes marriage as "being under somebody's thumb," says, "It will please her for you to think about her name. Nobody ever calls her by it now." Although relegated to subordinate roles, these women are initially presented favorably; but, by the end of the novel, Cather simultaneously praises Ántonia's role as mother and demeans the value of their independent lives.

In her concluding gesture, Cather offers a final obeisance to convention. Her description of Lena and Tiny undercuts their achievement and portrays them as stereotypical "old maids" who have paid for their refusal of their "natural" function. Thus, Tiny has become a "thin, hard-faced woman, very well dressed, very reserved," and something of a miser: she says "frankly that nothing interested her much now but making money." Moreover, Tiny has suffered the "mutilation" of her "pretty little feet"— the price of her unnatural success in the Klondike. Though a little more subtly, Lena is similarly disfigured, physically distorted by her emotional abberation. Jim presents her as crude and overblown in a final snapshot: "A comely woman, a trifle too plump, in a hat a trifle too large." So it is, too, with their friendship. Jim's barren account stresses unpleasantness about clothes and money and implies that an edge of bitterness has appeared. So much for female independence and success; so much for bonds between women. Cather, through Jim's account of them, has denigrated Tiny and Lena and their considerable achievement. In betraying these characters, versions of herself, Cather reveals the extent of her self-division.

Equally revealing is the transformation of Ántonia in the concluding segment. Now forty-four, she is the mother of eleven children, a grandmother without her former beauty. So changed is she that Jim at first fails to recognize her. She is "grizzled," "flat-chested," "toothless," and "battered", consumed by her life of childbearing and field work. The archetypal mother, Ántonia now signifies nourishment, protection, fertility, growth, and abundance: energy in service to the patriarchy, producing not "Ántonia's children" but "Cuzak's boys" (despite the fact that five of the children mentioned—Nina, Yulka, Martha, Anna, and Lucie—are girls). Like Cather's chapter title, Jim recognizes only the male children in his fantasy of eternal boyhood adventure, forgetting that in an earlier, less conventional and more androgynous world, his companion had been a girl—Ántonia herself.

Now Ántonia is glorified as a mythic source of life. Not only the progenitor of a large, vigorous family, she is also the source of the fertility and energy that have transformed the barren Nebraska prairie into a rich and fruitful garden. From her fruit cellar cavern pour forth into the light ten tumbling children—and the earth's abundance as well. In the images of this conclusion, she, no longer a woman, becomes Nature, a cornucopia, a "mine of life." Representing for Jim "immemorial human attitudes" which "fire the imagination," she becomes an idea and disappears under a symbolic weight, leaving for his friends and companions her highly individualized male children.

The conclusion of *My Ántonia* has usually been read as a triumph of the pioneer woman: Ántonia has achieved victory over her own hard early life and over the forces of Nature which made an immense struggle of farm life in Nebraska. But in fact, as we have seen, Cather and her narrator celebrate one of our most familiar stereotypes, one that distorts and reduces the lives of women. The image of the earth mother, with its implicit denial of Ántonia's individual identity, mystifies motherhood and nurturing while falsely promising fulfillment. Here Cather has found the means to glorify and dispose of Ántonia simultaneously, and she has done so in a way that is consonant with our stereotypical views and with her own psychological exigencies. The image of Ántonia that Cather gives us at the novel's conclusion is one that satisfies our national longings as well: coming to us from an age which gave us Mother's Day, it is hardly surprising that *My Ántonia* has lived on as a celebration of the pioneer woman's triumph and as a paean to the fecundity of the American woman and American land.

Cather's career illustrates the strain that women writers have endured and to which many besides Cather have succumbed. In order to create independent and heroic women, women who are like herself, the woman writer must avoid male identification, the likelihood of which is enhanced by being a writer who is unmarried, childless, and a lesbian. In the case of *My Ántonia*, Cather had to contend not only with the anxiety of creating a strong woman character, but also with the fear of a homosexual attraction to Annie/Ántonia. The novel's defensive narrative structure, the absence of thematic and structural unity that readers have noted, these are the results of such anxieties. Yet, because it has been difficult for readers to recognize the betrayal of female independence and female sexuality in fiction—their absence is customary—it has also been difficult to penetrate the ambiguities of *My Ántonia*, a crucial novel in Cather's long writing career.

Chronology

1873	Born December 7, near Winchester, Virginia, to Charles F. Cather and Mary Virginia Boak Cather. Willa was to be the oldest of seven children.
1884	Moves with her parents to a ranch in Webster County, Nebraska.
1885	Family moves to Red Cloud, Nebraska.
1890	Cather moves to Lincoln to complete preparation for entering the University of Nebraska.
1891–95	Attends University of Nebraska, paying her way by working as a newspaper columnist during her two final years.
1895–96	Stays at home in Red Cloud.
1896–97	Goes to Pittsburgh to work as a magazine editor.
1897–1901	Works as newspaper editor and drama reviewer for Pittsburgh's *Daily Leader*.
1901–2	Teaches English and Latin at Central High School in Pittsburgh.
1903	*April Twilights* (a book of poems).
1903–6	Teaches at Allegheny High in Pittsburgh.
1905	*The Troll Garden* (short stories).
1906–12	Moves to New York City to join editorial staff of *McClure's Magazine*.
1908	Moves into apartment with Edith Lewis, subsequently her lifelong companion.
1912	*Alexander's Bridge* (her first published novel).
1913	*O, Pioneers!*
1915	*The Song of the Lark.*
1918	*My Ántonia.*
1920	*Youth and the Bright Medusa* (stories).
1922	*One of Ours.*

1923   *A Lost Lady.*
1925   *The Professor's House.*
1927   *Death Comes for the Archbishop.*
1931   *Shadows on the Rock.*
1932   *Obscure Destinies* (stories).
1935   *Lucy Gayheart.*
1936   *Not Under Forty* (essays).
1940   *Sapphira and the Slave Girl.*
1947   Dies at her home in New York City on April 24.
1948   *The Old Beauty* (stories).
1949   *Willa Cather on Writing* (essays).

Contributors

HAROLD BLOOM, Sterling Professor of the Humanities at Yale University, is the author of *The Anxiety of Influence, Poetry and Repression,* and many other volumes of literary criticism. His forthcoming study, *Freud: Transference and Authority,* attempts a full-scale reading of all of Freud's major writings. A MacArthur Prize Fellow, he is general editor of five series of literary criticism published by Chelsea House.

DAVID DAICHES is Regius Professor of English Emeritus at the University of Edinburgh. His books include studies of Willa Cather and Robert Burns and *The Novel in the Modern World.*

JAMES E. MILLER, JR., is Professor of English at the University of Chicago. He has written widely upon American literature, upon Walt Whitman in particular.

ROBERT E. SHOLES is Professor of English at Brown University. His literary criticism includes *Structuralism in Literature* and *Semiotics and Interpretation.*

DOROTHY VAN GHENT, who taught at the Universities of Montana and Vermont as well as Brandeis and Harvard, was the author of *The English Novel: Form and Function.*

WALLACE STEGNER, Emeritus Professor of English at Stanford University, is the author of many works of fiction including *The Gallery of Zion, Angle of Repose, Big Rock Candy Mountain,* and *One Way to Spell Man.*

TERENCE MARTIN teaches English at Indiana University. His books include *Nathaniel Hawthorne* and *Instructed Vision,* a study of the influence of Scottish philosophy upon the origins of American fiction.

DAVID STOUCK teaches English at Simon Fraser University in Vancouver. He has written several works about Willa Cather.

135

BLANCHE H. GELFANT is Professor of English at Dartmouth College. She is the author of *The American City Novel* and *American Women Writing*.

EVELYN HELMICK is Academic Dean at Salem College. She has written on Emerson and on Willa Cather.

DEBORAH G. LAMBERT teaches English at Merrimack Valley College in North Andover, Massachusetts.

Bibliography

Allen, Edward. "Willa Cather's Novels of the Frontier: A Study in Thematic Symbolism." *American Literature* 13, no. 1 (1949):71–93.

Bennett, Mildred. *The World of Willa Cather*. Lincoln: University of Nebraska Press, 1961.

Bloom, Lillian D., and Edward Allen. *Willa Cather's Gift of Sympathy*. Carbondale: Southern Illinois University Press, 1962.

Brown, E. K. "Homage to Willa Cather." *Yale Review* 36 (1946):77–92.

———. *Willa Cather, A Critical Biography*. Completed by Leon Edel. New York: Knopf, 1953.

———. "Willa Cather and the West." *University of Toronto Quarterly* 5 (1936):544–66.

Cather, Willa. *Willa Cather on Writing*. New York, Knopf, 1949.

Cooperman, Stanley. "Willa Cather and the Bright Face of Death." *Literature and Psychology* 12, no. 1 (1963):81–87.

Daiches, David. *Willa Cather, A Critical Introduction*. Ithaca, N.Y.: Cornell University Press, 1951.

Edel, Leon. "Willa Cather's *The Professor's House:* An Inquiry into the Use of Psychology in Literary Criticism." *Literature and Psychology* 4, no. 5 (1954):69–79.

Fryer, Judith. "Cather's Felicitous Space." *The Prairie Schooner* 55, nos. 1–2 (1981):185–97.

Gerber, Philip L. *Willa Cather*. Boston: Twayne, 1975.

Greene, George. "Willa Cather's Grand Manan." *The Prairie Schooner* 55, nos.1–2 (1981):233–40.

Jessup, Josephine Luire. *The Faith of Our Feminists: A Study in the Novels of Edith Wharton, Ellen Glasgow and Willa Cather*. New York: R. R. Smith, 1950.

Lewis, Edith. *Willa Cather Living: A Personal Record*. New York: Knopf, 1953.

McFarland, Dorothy Tuck. *Willa Cather*. New York: Ungar, 1972.

Miller, Bruce E. "The Testing of Willa Cather's Humanism: *A Lost Lady* and Other Cather Novels." *Kansas Quarterly* 5, no. 4 (1973):43–49.

Murphy, John J., ed. *Five Essays on Willa Cather, the Merrimack Symposium*. Andover, Mass.: Merrimack College, 1974.

Randall, John Herman. *The Landscape and the Looking Glass: Willa Cather's Search for Value*. Boston: Houghton Mifflin, 1960.

Rapin, René. *Willa Cather*. New York: R. M. McBride, 1930.

Rosowski, Susan J. "Willa Cather—A Pioneer in Art." *The Prairie Schooner* 55, nos. 1–2 (1981):141–54.

Rucker, Mary E. "Prospective Focus in *My Ántonia*." *Arizona Quarterly* 29 (1973):303–16.

Sergeant, Elizabeth Shepley. *Willa Cather, A Memoir*. Philadelphia: Lippincott, 1953.

Shroeter, James. *Willa Cather and Her Critics*. Ithaca: Cornell University Press, 1967.

Slote, Bernice. "An Exploration of Cather's Early Writing." *Great Plains Quarterly* 2, no. 4 (1982):210–17.

———. "Willa Cather's Sense of History." *Women, Women Writers and the West*. Edited by L. L. Lee and Merrill Lewis. Troy, N.Y.: Whitson, 1979.

Stouck, David. "Marriage and Friendship in *My Ántonia*." *Great Plains Quarterly* 2, no. 4 (1982):224–31.

———. *Willa Cather's Imagination*. Lincoln: University of Nebraska Press, 1975.

———. "Willa Cather's Unfurnished Novel: Narrative in Perspectives." *Wascana Review* 6, no. 4 (1972):41–51.

Stuckey, William J. "*My Ántonia*: A Rose For Miss Cather." *Studies in the Novel* 4 (1972):473–81.

Turner, Frederick Jackson. *The Frontier in American History*. New York: Henry Holt, 1920.

Van Doren, Carl. "Willa Cather." In *American Novel*, 281–93. New York: Macmillan, 1921.

Van Ghent, Dorothy. *Willa Cather*. Minneapolis: University of Minnesota Press, 1964.

Woodress, James. *Willa Cather: Her Life and Her Art*. Lincoln: University of Nebraska Press, 1970.

Acknowledgments

"Decline of the West" by David Daiches from *Willa Cather: A Critical Introduction* by David Daiches, © 1951 by Cornell University. Reprinted by permission of Cornell University Press.

"*My Ántonia:* A Frontier Drama of Time" by James E. Miller, Jr., from *American Quarterly* 10, no. 4 (Winter 1958), © 1958 by the American Studies Association. Reprinted by permission of the author and *American Quarterly*.

"Hope and Memory in *My Ántonia*" by Robert E. Scholes from *Shenandoah* 14, no. 1 (Autumn 1962), © 1962 by Washington and Lee University. Reprinted by permission of the author and the Editor of *Shenandoah*.

"Willa Cather" by Dorothy Van Ghent from *Willa Cather* (*Pamphlets of American Writers,* no. 36) by Dorothy Van Ghent, © 1964 by the University of Minnesota. Reprinted by permission of the University of Minnesota Press.

"Willa Cather, *My Ántonia*" by Wallace Stegner from *The American Novel from James Fenimore Cooper to William Faulkner,* edited by Wallace Stegner, © 1965 by Basic Books, Inc., Publishers. Reprinted by permission of the publisher.

"The Drama of Memory in *My Ántonia*" by Terence Martin from *PMLA* 84, no. 2 (March 1969), © 1969 by the Modern Language Association of America. Reprinted by permission of the Modern Language Association of America.

"Perspective as Structure and Theme in *My Ántonia*" by David Stouck from *Texas Studies in Literature and Language* 12, no. 2 (Summer 1970), © 1970 by the University of Texas Press. Reprinted by permission.

"The Forgotten Reaping-Hook: Sex in *My Ántonia*" by Blanche H. Gelfant from *American Literature* 43, no. 1 (March 1971), © 1971 by Duke University Press. Reprinted by permission.

"*My Ántonia* and the American Dream" by James E. Miller, Jr., from *Prairie Schooner* 48, no. 2 (Spring 1974), © 1974 by the University of Nebraska Press. Reprinted by permission.

"The Mysteries of Ántonia" by Evelyn Helmick from *The Midwest Quarterly* 17, no. 2 (January 1976), © 1976 by *The Midwest Quarterly*. Reprinted by permission of *The Midwest Quarterly*, Pittsburgh State University, Pittsburgh, Kansas.

"The Defeat of a Hero: Autonomy and Sexuality in *My Ántonia*" by Deborah G. Lambert from *American Literature* 53, no. 4 (January 1982), © 1982 by Duke University Press. Reprinted by permission.

Index